Meriden – Nr. Coventry

A big thank-you to everyone who came to the Sylvia Bishop weekend course in Birmingham. The venue was supposed to be heated, but it turned out to be bitterly cold. It just shows how good Sylvia is – that people stayed on the first day and came back on the second day. What a compliment to Sylvia's phenomenal abilit...

Basingstoke

May I through DTW pass on to Sylvia all the thank-yous of those who attended a most enjoyable and informative weekend. No problem went unsolved, no question unanswered. So impressed with Sylvia's training methods were those who attended the course that I was inundated with requests for a repeat course, which was booked there and then for November 1984. Dogs that had gone dead bounced like pups, dogs and handlers came away fitter, keener and more controlled. Everyone agreed the course was sheer 'MAGIC'.

Billingshurst D.T.C.

May I, through the pages of DTW, thank Sylvia Bishop for the second Handlers' Course she gave. Like the first one, the difficult bit was in getting Sylvia to break for tea or to go home. I know everyone enjoyed it, they are already asking for an encore.

Idle, Bradford

The help and advice given on one of her courses is absolutely amazing, the results you can hardly believe, especially when you see the dogs are actually enjoying themselves, which is what Obedience is supposed to be all about...

Carterton, Oxford

In saying that Sylvia is a warm and generous lady I am in the most part preaching to the converted. But I am going to tell you how great she really is. During the Course I mentioned how disappointed my husband was at having to miss it, and as there were several Obedience lads out in the Falklands with my husband, how I wished it had been possible to have Videoed the course to send to them. I couldn't believe my ears when she offered to lend me one to send to the Falklands for the lads. We had never even met before and there she was offering to lend me, a perfect stranger, one of her own precious videos to send all those thousands of miles. It was incredible. Two weeks later at Stoneleigh Show I was given not one, but two to send, one training and the other the whole of Crufts Obedience. How is that for trust and generosity?

By courtesy of Dog Training Weekly

Sylvia Bishop with 'Jess'
Obedience Champion Enchanted Blue Star

'Jess' to whom the book is dedicated

IT'S MAGIC

Training your dog
with Sylvia Bishop

Crufts 1985
Best of luck for the
Sylvia Ann Bishop

Ready, Steady, Let's go!

IT'S MAGIC

Training your dog with Sylvia Bishop

A COMPLETE MANUAL

The step by step guide to dog training

PHOTOGRAPHY
BY BARRY SMITH,
PHOTOGRAPHIAN

Published by Sylvia Bishop
Produced by Barry Smith of Photographian
First edition 1985

Photographic processing by Colortech of Worthing
Filmset and printed in Great Britain by
BAS Printers Limited, Over Wallop, Hampshire

ISBN 0 9510143 0 7

Contents

Forewords

'It's Magic' is an extremely apt phrase to use as the title for this fascinating, interesting and informative book.

All Mrs Bishop's dogs are very happy as her training is done entirely by persuasion with no harshness at all.

Her 'Retrieve' is something quite different to the method that anyone else has used and taught in the past. The fact that so many people are benefitting by her teaching is 'proof of the pudding'.

She has laid out very clearly in her Introduction everything that all dog lovers, whether or not they are in the 'Obedience World', would be well advised to read. Indeed I can think of many a dog who would benefit by a little training from her!

She started her first weekend training course in 1974 and has never looked back.

During those ten years, six of them have been spent in writing this book. Surely this must show that it is not just a spur of the moment whim to write a 'Best Seller'.

For me, merely a dog breeder of some thirty years, I found the whole book fascinating and very easy to follow and I am sure many others like me, as well as the Obedience fraternity, will find it very interesting and most instructive.

Mary Forwood
October 1984

Over the last 35 years no more than a dozen people have stood out above the rest as really great trainers and natural handlers, and these people have proved their worth by making three, four or five very different dogs into Obedience Champions.

Into this super group I would now certainly add the name of Sylvia Bishop, who, in my opinion, is one of today's stars both in the ring working her own dogs, and as an Instructor whose first priority is that the lessons for both handler and dog should be fun and enjoyed together.

In this book Sylvia has put her method into print and I am sure that all handlers and dogs will benefit from her fun and games way of training and develop a better understanding of each other, whether they are pet owners who need to learn the basics or competitive minded handlers striving for the top.

An excellent book that all can enjoy.

Muriel Pearce

Acknowledgements

I wish to express my thanks to the following individuals without whom this book would not have been completed. Angela Sanders, who, in spite of her statement that it would not be possible to capture the essence of my manner of training in writing, did nevertheless succeed in describing my methods of training; and her daughter Rachel who helped in so many ways.

Mary Forwood and Muriel Pearce for their Forewords.

My husband Roy and my family and my brother Michael for all their support and encouragement.

All my friends in the Obedience World for their support.

A special thanks to Ian, who, following all Angela's hard work, took all the photographs, spent so much of his spare time working with me to produce the book, and in so doing made it 'come alive'.

Glossary

Classes

Beginner
Novice
Test 'A'
Test 'B'
Test 'C'
Championship 'C'

Championship shows

To qualify to work at championship level one's dog has to qualify through the lower classes from beginners to open class 'C'.

There are, on average, 40 championship shows each year awarding tickets to qualify your dog and bitch for Crufts.

Open shows

Non-championship status.

OB. CH.

Obedience champion – to achieve this title a dog has to win three championship 'C' classes under three different judges not losing more than ten points out of a total of 300.

G.S.D.

German Shepherd Dog, previously called an alsatian.

W.S.D.

Working Sheep Dog.

Mouthing

A dog that chews a retrieve article.

Present.

Pronounced as to present something to someone.

Swivel

This means take your weight on your left foot and turn backwards so that you return to the heel position, this means that the exercise ends with the dog in the heel position without him always carrying out a finish.

Author's Preface

As far back as I can remember dogs have been part of my life. My whole family have been involved with dogs in one way or another. After leaving school I worked with Greyhounds, Great Danes, Spaniels and Alsatians (now known as German Shepherd Dogs). After my marriage my husband Roy trained and worked Jack Russels and Labradors for Rough Shooting during which time I was training Alsatians for Guard work.

It was as a result of taking an Alsatian to Road Safety classes that I was first introduced to the World of Obedience. At these classes I met Bob Follows who was to play an important part in my life because of his own interest in the Dog Obedience World. It was at this time that I first came into contact with working Sheepdogs or, as they are often termed, Border Collies.

I was totally fascinated by the way these pretty little dogs worked; they were so attentive and close to their handlers. One of these was a pretty Blue Merle Bitch called Jess and when, some months later, Bob Follows turned up with three four-month-old puppies from this Bitch I could not resist having one.

Against my husband Roy's and Bob's advice I chose a very nervous smooth-coated Blue Merle, looking more like a whippet than a collie, to be my first Obedience Dog. I called her Jess.

I totally disregarded my strongly held beliefs about avoiding a nervous puppy and let my heart rule my head. I have never regretted it. Jess 'Obedience Champion Enchanted Blue Star' opened the door to the world of Competitive Obedience and in so doing completely changed my life.

I will always remember when Charlie Wyant, that well known and respected personality of the Obedience World, first judged my beloved Jess as a baby of nine months. Afterwards he wrote 'a team that will go far'. I had no idea at that time how true his words would prove.

By twenty-two months Jess had qualified for Championship Classes, and not long after gaining her qualifiers she gave me the greatest thrill so far in our career by winning her first Championship ticket at Leicester on November the 3rd, 1973, under Jim Bombroff. It was the moment that most obedience handlers dream of – that elusive first prize which is the passport to the big ring at Crufts, the most coveted Dog Show in the World. It was one of the proudest moments in my life.

Jess went on to become a great champion and remained so until her retirement at Crufts in 1982. She had 134 trophies to her credit. She qualified for the big ring at Crufts for no less than ten consecutive years and in total she won 30 Challenge Certificates.

On the day she retired at Crufts the accolade she received from the spectators and her fellow competitors was the most moving of our career together.

This book is dedicated to 'Jess' who filled my life with so much joy. Regrettably she passed away on Tuesday the 28th August, 1984.

As all dog lovers will know, when this happens there is always a gap which can never be completely filled. Through this book her memory will live on.

However, happily I have three other dogs:
Obedience Champion Misty Magic – 'Misty'.
Obedience Champion Magic Sunday – 'Sunny' (Sunny is Misty's son).

Both of these are working sheepdogs.

The third is a German Shepherd Dog: Pajwie Crystal Gail – 'Cindy'. Although slower in obtaining good results she is nevertheless making nice progress, showing again that any breed can be successfully trained from 'puppyhood' by these methods.

There are many people in the world of dogs who in one way or another influence one's progress. One hopes to be a good pupil and ultimately emulate those one looks up to.

Over the years many top handlers have helped me and have watched my progress from the early days. To all those people I give my thanks.

There always will be obedience handlers who make it to the top and they are termed successful. But success should be measured by personal achievement by you and your dog and not by Rosettes. If you and your dog understand each other and give to each other in the ring, and outside it, THAT IS SUCCESS.

Introduction

This book is written for the benefit of both the ordinary pet dog owner and the pet owner who wishes to, or who already does, compete in Competitive Obedience.

Pet owners who wish to train their dog would find it beneficial to join a local dog club. Information about such clubs can be obtained from their local 'vet', the police, the local library or perhaps the local newspapers.

These classes will assist you to train your dog and give you an opportunity to socialise him with other dogs. They also provide contact with experienced dog owners who will discuss with you your pet's general care, e.g. Feeding, Worming and Grooming. If you have accepted the responsibility of an adult dog you may well have behavioural problems which will need correcting and a discussion about such problems with other club members is often valuable.

It may be at a later date you will decide to compete in Obedience Competitions. Your dog club will be able to give you all the information you need to do this. The club members will be able to explain the different types of shows and advise you about how to enter a show. I am also sure that there will be someone willing to take you to your first show and show you the 'ropes'.

My aim in writing this book is to try and set down the methods of training which will enable you to have not just a well trained dog but a keen happy worker ready to give you years of enjoyment in any sphere of competitive dog training, or pleasure in having a trained companion. The basic methods in this book are like a straight road with various types of dogs and handlers falling on either side and you the handler must make any slight adjustments necessary to accommodate these differences. The basic methods which you will find in the following chapters are written with the training of puppies in mind.

However my methods can be used for the older dog but the application of these methods may not be so straightforward because of bad habits or fears which an older dog may have acquired.

The whole essence of my method is total control without suppression of the dog's character. It is very easy to train a dog by total domination, that is by using a check chain and force; but whilst this produces results it does not produce the keenness or what I always refer to as 'THE WANT'.

I firmly believe that dogs, like humans, come nearer to reaching their full potential if they receive early stimulation. Therefore in order to reach a higher plane of achievement I hold the view that your puppy's training should start whilst the brain is still developing and I would advise everyone to commence training within the first week of ownership, even as young as six weeks. In this situation the handler must get down onto the floor. In fact must get down to the puppy's level both mentally and physically.

The principles to which I adhere are:

1 Learning through play with excitement and praise.

2 Never asking the dog to do anything more than he is capable of which means always proceeding at a pace suitable to his mental and physical development. This does not mean that you cannot teach more than one exercise at a time but that each exercise must be taught in stages and there must not be progress from one stage to the next until each one is clearly understood by the dog.

(Stage by stage learning guarantees that the dog will not be unduly pressurised, because you will not progress unless the dog understands everything that has been asked of him.)

3 Avoid confusion by telling your dog what you are going to do and by using the minimum number of commands.

For example: most people with their first dog will inform their dog that they are going for a walk before they are taken out. Eventually after constant repetition some dogs will go to the door and some will fetch their leads showing by their response that they understand what is going to happen.

In the same way I say we are going to do 'Heelwork' or 'Sendaways' etc. In time the dog will position himself ready for the exercise. This way the amount of handling is kept to a minimum and the dog is ready to respond before the actual command. There are eleven basic actions by the dog which require commands. These are: SIT, STAND, DOWN, HOLD, COME, STRAIGHT, CLOSE, LOOK, GO or AWAY, WATCH, CONTROL.

Any other commands are superfluous.

Important attributes for a dog trainer are patience and a sense of timing with quick reactions. The first is self explanatory, the second attribute is essential if the dog is to know by praise or correction when he is right or wrong. Praise is vital but it must be genuine; a dog is not fooled by pretence. The command and response MUST go together with praise. Every 'good' action your puppy does, even everyday actions, must be followed *immediately* with praise. Go overboard with praise, using such phrases as 'what a super puppy', 'clever dog', and 'brilliant puppy' said in really excited voice.

Every dog has to be disciplined but until the dog's or puppy's understanding is such that it knows *without a doubt* what is wanted of it no correction should be used. It is in this context that the greatest patience is required. At first any deserved correction should be verbal such as 'what are you doing' or 'think about it' in a gruff tone of voice. If that is insufficient one can escalate to a shake by the scruff on the neck or a shake accompanied by an eye to eye stare and on rare occasions with a very difficult dog perhaps a nip on the ear. All these simulate the correction which would be given by the pack leader. The degree of correction must be estimated correctly for each dog. Too little is ineffective; too much would cause the dog to cower and become worried. Correction during training must be given whilst the dog is being placed in the correct position with praise following *immediately*. No correction should be given whilst you are away from your dog, e.g., if your dog breaks a stay position do not shout at him from a distance but return quickly to his side and correct him.

Choosing Your Dog

One frequently reads that when choosing a dog you should first pick a breed suitable for the work to be undertaken and then consider the temperaments of the parents and the puppy. However most obedience dogs are pets and therefore I believe that the first thing you should do is to take a long hard look at yourself and your family.

As well as having a basically similar appearance each breed has a basic type of personality and within that type there are differences of temperament.

First and foremost, therefore, you should choose a breed which you like *living with.* For this I think you should consider Personality and Appearance as well as size and amount of care required, e.g., Grooming, Feeding and Exercise. You must also consider your family situation. For example, you would have problems if you had a highly excitable dog with highly excitable children living with elderly nervous grand-parents.

When you have decided which breeds you and your family can enjoy living with then select from those breeds one most suited for the job you want it to do.

Now is the time to consider temperament. NO, NOT THE DOG'S, YOURS. It is not only dogs who have different temperaments; human beings have quite a variety. They can be Aggressive, Amenable, Dominant, Submissive, Excitable, Calm, Confident, Nervous.

If you are aggressively dominant steer clear of a dog with a nervous disposition as you will 'flatten' it, but you could do well with an excitable confident dog. However, if you are dominant but calm you could cope with an anxious dog as your positive but calm approach would give him confidence.

A nervous and anxious dog would not succeed with a nervous or excitable person. Such a person needs a calm confident dog.

Take time in selecting your breed and even more time in choosing the breed line.

When choosing a dog for obedience competition most people these days choose collies which to my mind is a shame. They are in my opinion more intelligent than any other breed and are therefore quite complex. Collies need careful handling and for every one that makes it happily through the obedience classes there are fifty who do not. German Shepherd Dogs are slowly disappearing from the obedience scene, partly because they are slower to mature and therefore cannot be rushed through the training and partly because some training methods make them bored and unwilling.

Golden Retrievers are very under-rated. They are intelligent, although stubborn, and slow to mature. Alas when looking for an obedience competition dog most people overlook these beautiful dogs.

There are hundreds of breeds from which to choose. The choice is yours. If you have a breed other than a collie don't think that it has to be trained in a different way. Only the pace of training need be different.

Equipment

There is so much equipment on the market from which to choose that by and large I think it is a matter of personal preference.

However I am very much against young dogs being put on a slip collar and in particular a chain slip collar or choke as it used to be called. In my experience the chain slip collar is *very rarely* used correctly and becomes a training hindrance rather than a training aid. When a chain slip collar is used badly training becomes nothing but punishment for the dog and all enjoyment is lost. Occasionally with a difficult adult dog there may be good reason to change to such a collar but as a general rule they are unnecessary.

One type of collar that is useful is the limited slip collar. This is basically a leather or material collar with a piece of chain joining the two ends instead of a buckle. The lead is attached to the chain and when pulled the collar tightens up to a limited degree. This has the advantage that if the dog pulls away from the handler he cannot slip his head out of the collar.

Personally I use an ordinary leather collar and lead but for adult dogs I frequently use a thin *soft flat* cord. There have been hundreds of dogs up and down the country trained successfully on these and they have many advantages. They do not make an unpleasant noise or break the dog's fur. They slip easily and there are no heavy clips to bang around the dog's face.

The Early Days

Pack animals living under natural conditions begin learning all they need to know for survival from about six weeks of age.

All the time they are playing with their litter mates and their parents they are learning. At first they rough each other up fairly gently, nipping at each other's neck, face, ears and legs. This play gradually escalates until it becomes quite fierce. This does two things; it determines a pecking order in the litter and it is the basis of their prey catching and killing. Also from about six weeks of age the parents discipline their young. As with the play the discipline is gentle at first, e.g., a slight growl, but it becomes more forceful as the puppies mature mentally and physically.

The domestic dog behaves in the same way during it's early months of life therefore when you take your puppy home you must become a substitute parent and playmate. Instead of aimlessly playing with my puppies I channel this play into teaching (without pressure) the responses to various commands, thus maximising during these early days on the propensity the young dog has for learning. The puppy also learns that I am the pack leader.

Having given your puppy a day or two to settle in, put a collar on him and leave it on no matter how he reacts to it. When he becomes indifferent to the collar, attach a light lead to it and let the puppy pull around on it for a few moments then take it off and fuss him.

Gradually increase the time that he spends playing on the lead until he plays in a relaxed way with the lead on. It is important that the puppy adjusts to a collar and lead early and that his early experiences of both are pleasant because these two articles will become the extension of your arm and hand, and will be used for training and not only for taking your dog for a walk.

I strongly recommend that you ask your veterinary surgeon to give your puppy temporary vaccinations so that as soon as possible and as soon as he has adjusted to the collar and lead you can take him out. It has been shown by various researchers' work into dog behaviour that the early experiences of a puppy leave the most lasting impressions, therefore if a puppy can have early *pleasant* experiences of as many situations as possible he will be more likely to face strange situations with equanimity throughout his life. Therefore I suggest that before he is three months old you introduce your puppy to as many humans, dogs and other animals as possible and let him experience busy shopping centres and noisy traffic; but make sure that these experiences are not frightening. Every day spend time handling and talking to your puppy. Play with him, stroke him, love him. Get to know his personality and his temperament by watching his reactions to various types of play and various situations. Is he timid or bold, is he a thinker or one who charges at new situations like a bull at a gate? Is he dominant, does he growl when you touch the food he is eating? Watching his habits; does he readily sit or prefer to lie down? Does he bark? It is important for you to *know* your puppy so that you can train accordingly, encouraging the good traits, discouraging the bad.

Very young puppies need long periods of sleep and short periods of 'play learning' plus food and warmth. When your puppy wakes from a sleep put him out to be clean and then play and train and after this feed him and let him rest or relax in his own way. Never ask your puppy to 'play-learn' when he wants to be quiet.

When playing with your puppy get down to his level. *Get on to the floor*. Never bend over him; this will make him feel vulnerable. At first gently poke and pull the puppy around, gently pull on the collar, push him away clap your hands and call him back. Throw soft toys for him, play 'tug of war' with socks. Grab at him gently, pinch his loose flesh, grab at his legs and his tail. In fact try to play with him as if you were another dog but bear in mind that you are much bigger and stronger.

Incorporate the lead into the play; roll the puppy away from you and gently pull him back to you at the same time saying the word 'Come'. Let the puppy chew and bite the lead in the same way as he chews and bites your hands in play. This is how the puppy learns to enjoy the lead, even though being on the lead means that the puppy is under your control. Choose a toy that will be suitable to use in training and get your puppy keen on it. I always use a small piece of carpet but anything small and tough which the dog enjoys will do equally well.

Every dog owner uses the dog's name and he soon learns that it means 'Pay attention' as something else will follow. In the same way he can learn the meaning of other words. From the word go, give a word of command to any natural action that you think is clever or useful, so that every time the puppy does something naturally he hears the same word. For example, every time he lays down say a word such as 'settle' or 'bed', and in time you will be able to use this word in order to get him to lie down quietly. When the puppy sits say 'sit'. When you are putting him into a car say 'in the car'. When you are going to do something like going to the park or giving the puppy his food tell him, give it a word or phrase.

When I throw my puppy's carpet for him to fetch I say 'Kill it' and then have a tug of war. This then becomes my release word. This way, by constant repetition and without force or pressure, the dog slowly builds up a vocabularly.

Whilst you are getting to know your puppy he is getting to know and respect you. He will learn that you provide food and that you can take food or anything else away from him. He will learn that you are his playmate but you are also the pack leader. He will learn to understand your different tones of voice and your different moods and react accordingly. If he has a dominant character and growls if you take something away from him you must show that you are the boss, gently shake him and say 'What are you doing?', take the food or article, fuss him, and then give it back. Do this every day until the puppy accepts your dominance without demur because he will expect you to be in control at all times and will only feel secure as long as you are.

This understanding of each other is the foundation of a good relationship. This relationship is formed during the first weeks that you and your puppy are together, so *Don't waste them.*

PLAY IS VITAL FOR MY METHOD OF TRAINING. Learning through play is not only pleasant for both of you but the lessons learned are retained for longer, so never cease to play with your dog.

How to use this Book

This book is a teach yourself course in dog training for anyone and everyone, whether you just want a happily trained dog as a pet or to enter the Obedience World from local dog shows through to Crufts. The most important thing to remember is that Sylvia's methods, which are unique, do work.

Every dog loves to play, so in a subtle way you can incorporate all the training around the play sessions. This way, from the dog's point of view, the exercises become fun lessons. That is the secret of the success of Sylvia's methods. Thousands of people have already benefitted by these methods taught by Sylvia at courses throughout the country. She also runs a dog training centre mid week.

You must start at the beginning and work methodically and patiently through every stage of the exercises. Only move on to the next stage when the previous exercise is completely understood by you and your dog.

Work through the book at a pace which suits both you and your dog. As you progress from page to page many of the steps and photographs are repeated. This has been designed deliberately firstly to assist you to remember each step, and secondly, to avoid the need to keep turning back the pages.

Remember it does work, but be patient and if you are starting from scratch do not be tempted to jump the pages.

The very first exercise, which you should start teaching during your playtime with your puppy, begins with the instruction for you to get down on the floor to play with your puppy.

For the benefit of the elderly or the disabled who might find this difficult or impractical the illustrations show the puppy being taught on a table top.

In fact Sylvia did train her own Chihuahua in this method.

It is advised that you read the complete book and study the 13 chapters of exercises before you commence your training programme.

There are spaces throughout the book for your own pencilled notes.

Some of the photographs show people, other dogs and sometimes vehicles. It is advised that you train your dog in this sort of environment where possible, in order that he gets used to working where there are distractions.

Pajwie Crystal Gail 'Cindy'

Sylvia Bishop with her 'Family'

The exercise of Distant Control as laid down for Class 'C' by the Kennel Club in January 1985 is as follows:
The dog to sit, stand and down at a marked place not less than ten paces from handler in any order, on command from judge to handler. Six instructions to be given in the same order for each dog. Excessive movement, i.e. more than the length of the dog, in any direction by the dog, having regard to its size, will be penalised. The dog shall start the exercise with its front feet behind a designated point. No penalty for excessive movement in a forward direction shall be imposed until the back legs of the dog pass the designated point.

By courtesy of the Kennel Club.

1

Control

Leading to Distant Control

Control is the basis for all dog training. When I give the command 'Control' I expect my dogs to stop immediately and remain stationary watching and listening for the next command.

Therefore the importance of 'Distant Control' lies in the dog's response to the word 'Control'. If the response is correct this will give you immediate control in any exercise or in any everyday situation. Distant control also teaches the dog the correct response to the basic commands of 'Sit', 'Stand', and 'Down'. The element of the exercises requiring commands at a distance is unimportant as this will come automatically when the dog is mature and confident. For the Stand position I always use the command BACK preceded by the dog's name. In the early days Stand and Sit can be a little confusing. Always use the dog's name before the Stand position in order to get the dog's attention and have him ready to move.

Control

First Exercise

Start teaching this first exercise during your playtime with your puppy.

For the benefit of the elderly or the disabled who might find it difficult or impractical to get down on the floor, the illustrations show the puppy being taught on a table top. In fact I did train my own chihuahua in this method.

1 Play with your puppy, push him away from you and as he runs up to you stop him in his tracks by cupping your hands round his chest at the same time giving the command 'Control'. The puppy will probably sit but may just stand. →

Repeat of 1 shown on the floor.

Repeat of 2 shown on the floor. →

2 If the puppy sits immediately say 'Sit', if he remains standing give the command 'Sit' and at the same time push him back into the Sit position. Gently stroke and praise.

3 When he becomes restless put one hand under his body and raise backwards into the stand position giving the dog's name and the command 'Back'. Stroke and praise for a couple of seconds.

4 Release by gently pushing him backwards or by throwing his toy behind him and playing with that. INCORPORATE THIS INTO EVERY PLAY SESSION.

Notes

When the puppy responds to the words 'Control' and 'Sit' and moves into the Stand as soon as your hand moves towards his body, it is time to begin teaching this exercise standing up. This may be after weeks depending on the puppy.

Control

Second Exercise The 'Sit' to the 'Stand'

1 Stand with your dog on the lead and in the Sit position by your left hand side with the lead in your left hand.

2 Place your right hand under the dog's chin.

Give the command 'control' and swivel to the front.

At the same time mov your right hand from under the chin to the left side of the dog's face and

4 Walk round the dog keeping his head up with one hand under his chin and

use the other hand under the body to keep him in the stand.

This will necessitate changing over hands on the way round.

lace your left hand on
ne right side of the
og's face.

3 Give the dog's name and the command 'back'.

If the dog fails to move gently push him into the stand

with your foot under the centre of his body.

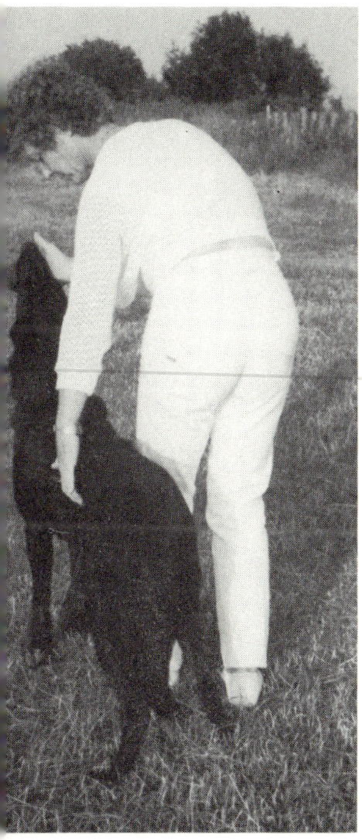

ently praise by voice
hilst you are moving.

5 Release by throwing his toy over his head and behind him and play.

This keeps the dog's head up, encouraging him to move into the backward position.

Notes

As this is a relatively static exercise it could easily become very boring for the dog. Therefore the play that follows the position must be profuse and exciting. If at any time the dog moves position repeat the word 'control' and place the dog in the required position. Do not progress to teaching a second position until the dog is absolutely reliable on the first.

Control

Third Exercise The 'Stand' to the 'Sit'

1 Stand with your dog on the lead and in the Stand position by your left hand side with the lead in your left hand.

2 Place your right hand under the dog's chin and giving the command 'Control' swivel to the front at the same time move your right hand

from under the chin to the left side of the dog's face and place your left hand on the right of the dog's face, gently stroking his head. →

round him at the same time quietly praising him.

Again this will necessitate changing

over hands on the way round. →

3 Give the command 'Sit' and gently pushing the head backwards into the shoulders push him into the 'Sit'.

Close up showing the hands.

4 Keep control of the dog with your hands, walk

5 Release by throwing his toy behind him and play.

Notes

Gradually combine these two positions until the dog has mastered the 'Sit' to the 'Stand' and the 'Stand' to the 'Sit'. When you are satisfied that your dog responds quickly and confidently to these two positions proceed to teach the next exercise The Down Position.

Control

Fourth Exercise Teaching the Down

1 Once more get down on the floor and play. Give the command 'Control' followed by the dog's name. Give the command 'Back' placing your dog in the Stand position. →

3 Give the command 'Down'

and with a firm downwards movement push the dog backwards into the Down position. →

Relax the dog by stroking his head in a soothing manner from the muzzle backwards to the ears and down to the shoulders.

2 When the dog is relaxed, manoeuvre the hands until the thumbs are in the hollow between the breast bone and the shoulders, with the fingers extended around the shoulders.

4 Praise and release quickly with much fuss and play as in this position the dog feels vulnerable and may fight against remaining down. Repeat two or three times at each session.

Notes

Once the dog is going down happily and remaining there proceed to carry out the next exercise, The 'Stand' to the 'Down' in a more formal manner.

Control

Fifth Exercise The Stand to the Down

1 Stand with your dog on the lead and in the stand position by your left hand side with the lead in your left hand.

2 As before, place your right hand under the dog's chin and giving the command 'Control' swivel to the front at the same time move your right hand from under the dog's →

4 Give the command 'Down'

and push the dog backwards into the Down position. →

chin to the left side of the dog's face and place your left hand on the right side of the dog's face. Remain in front of him for a few seconds gently stroking his head.

3 As before, place the hands so that the thumbs are in the hollow between the breast bone and the shoulders and the fingers extended over the shoulders.

5 Swivel to the heel position, keeping the dog's head up with your right hand.

6 Praise release and play.

Control

You can now combine the sit to the stand, the stand to the sit, the stand to the down, the down to the stand, and the down to the sit. When teaching this exercise never teach the dog to go from the *sit to the down*, as this may encourage forward movement.

Your aim must be to teach the dog to change positions with backward movements. Always taking the front feet back to the back feet when sitting, and moving the hind feet backwards into the stand. The down position should be achieved by lowering the front legs and shoulders before the hind-quarters; this is more desirable than achieving it via the sit as it will prevent any forward movement. Never give a second command. If the dog does not respond quickly place him in the position. If he moves give the command 'Control' and put him back into the correct position.

When you are sure that your dog fully understands the commands for CONTROL and when he obeys with keenness you can commence giving the commands from a distance.

Distant Control

The Sit to the Stand

1 Stand with your dog on the lead and in the sit position with the lead in your left hand, and his toy in your right hand.
2 Give the command 'Control'.
3 Go to the end of the lead facing the dog.
4 Give the dog's name and the command 'Back'.
5 Immediately walk towards your dog, walk on past him and round to the front, coming to a halt close to him.
6 Praise and release by throwing his toy over his head and behind him and play.

The Stand to the Sit

1 Stand with your dog on the lead and in the Stand position by your left hand side with the lead in your left hand.
2 Give the command 'Control'.
3 Go to the end of the lead facing the dog.
4 Give the command 'Sit'.
5 As before, immediately walk towards your dog, walk on past him and round to the front, coming to a halt close to him.
6 Praise release and play.

The Stand to the Down

1 Stand with your dog on the lead and in the Stand position by your left hand side with the lead in your left hand.
2 Give the command 'Control'.
3 Go to the end of the lead facing the dog.
4 Give the command 'Down'.
5 As before, immediately walk towards your dog, walk on past him and round to the front, coming to a halt close to him.
6 Praise release and play.

Continue in this manner always walking round the dog and releasing with play between each exercise position. Always commencing with the dog in the heel position and in the position that he has just left. If the dog fails to take up the required position instantly, do not re-command, but place him in that position. If at any time the dog attempts to move before being released, immediately replace him giving the command 'Control'.

Once you and your dog are confident, you can attempt walking straight round your dog to the end of the lead and give a second position before releasing him. Gradually increase the number of positions given before releasing. Never increase the number of positions if the dog does not remain keen and steady.

The next stage is to test the dog off the lead. Have him running free, call out 'Control' and give one position. If the dog responds it will show that he is mentally prepared to accept the discipline of control at a distance.

With the dog in the heel position and off the lead and with his toy in your right hand give the command 'Control', leave the dog and walk in front of the dog to a distance of about fifteen feet, turn and face the dog. Give the command for one position. Immediately walk forward and round the dog as before. Praise and release by throwing the toy over and behind the dog.

If your dog obeys the command it will show that your training has been good so stick to it.

Train less frequently now but keep the enjoyment in the exercises by always using the dog's toy to play with whenever he is released. Do not attempt to train in a formal way for the ring but train at random, sometimes giving just one position on it's own, sometimes several positions. Only occasionally give commands from a distance and sometimes go back to training on the lead.

For the Stay Exercises the dog is required to remain in an exact position until released.

The Kennel Club Regulations as laid down in January, 1985 are as follows:

The 'Sit' Stay. 'The Judge or Steward will direct handlers to positions in the ring. The command 'Last command' will be given when all are ready and handlers should then instantly give their final command to their dog. Any further commands or signals after this 'last command' will be penalised. Handlers will then be instructed to leave their dogs and walk to positions indicated until ordered to return to them. Dogs should remain at the sit position throughout the test. This is a group test and all dogs must compete together.'

The 'Stand' Stay and the 'Down' Stay should be carried out exactly as for the 'Sit' Stay.

By courtesy of the Kennel Club

2

The Stay Exercises

Reliable stays come with the dog having the confident knowledge that his owner will return. It is in order to ensure that the dog is relaxed and confident that I progress by very small steps, each exercise being only marginally more advanced than the previous one.

Progress through the following exercises at a pace suitable to your dog's age and capabilities. Do not rush through them as anxiety in the early days of learning will cause unreliability in your stays later on.

When teaching Stays always have the dog on the lead and never give more than one command to your dog. Any time your dog attempts to move return quickly to his side, take hold of the lead, and correct his position and then praise and release him. Do not shout corrections to your dog from a distance. The only time that commands should be given from a distance is during Distant Control and at the end of the Sendaway. I always train Stays on the lead so that if the dog moves I can take hold of the lead and do not have to make a grab at the dog.

The Sit Stay

First Exercise

1 With your dog on the lead place him sitting in the Heel position.
2 Give the command 'Sit'.
3 Count to ten.
4 Praise release and play.

Do not let your dog lay on you.

Immediately praise and release. Then start again. When the dog remains sitting happily for ten seconds proceed to:

Second Exercise

1 With your dog on the lead place him sitting in the Heel position.
2 Give the command 'Sit'.
3 Make forward and backward movements with your right leg for five seconds.
4 Praise release and play.

Third Exericise

1 With your dog on the lead place him sitting in the Heel position.
2 Give the command 'Sit'.
3 Take a very small step away from your dog.
4 Return to your dog's side after five seconds.
5 Praise release and play.

Fourth Exercise

1 With your dog on the lead place him sitting in the Heel position.
2 Give the command 'Sit'.
3 Take a very small step away from your dog.
4 Return to the dog's side after ten seconds.
5 Praise release and play.

Fifth Exercise

1 With your dog on the lead place him sitting in the Heel position.
2 Give him the command 'Sit'.
3 Take a step in front of your dog.
4 Return to the dog's side after ten seconds.
5 Praise release and play.

Sixth Exercise

1 With your dog on the lead place him sitting in the Heel position.
2 Give him the command 'Sit'.
3 Take a step behind your dog.
4 Return to the dog's side after ten seconds.
5 Praise release and play.

Seventh Exercise

1 With your dog on the lead place him sitting in the Heel position.
2 Give him the Command 'Sit'.
3 Walk a quarter of a circle round the front of your dog.
4 Return to the dog's side.
5 Praise release and play.

Eighth Exercise

1 With your dog on the lead place him sitting in the Heel position.
2 Give him the command 'Sit'.
3 Walk half a circle round the front of your dog.
4 Return to the dog's side.
5 Praise release and play.

Ninth Exercise

1 With the dog on the lead place him sitting in the Heel position.
2 Give him the command 'Sit'.
3 Walk a full circle round the dog.
4 Praise release and play.

Tenth Exercise

1 With the dog on the lead place him sitting in the Heel position.
2 Give the command 'Sit'.
3 Walk a full circle round your dog.
4 Praise and release.
5 Place the dog once more sitting in the Heel position.
6 Give the command 'Sit'.
7 Go to the end of the lead in front of the dog.
8 Very gently pull the lead. This will usually cause the dog to move. If he does, return to his side, replace him in the Sit position, then Praise and release. Return to step 1 and repeat the exercise.
9 If the dog remains sitting when you gently pull the lead, return to the dog's side.
10 Praise release and play.

Eleventh Exercise

1 With the dog on the lead place him sitting in the Heel position.
2 Give the command 'Sit'.
3 Take a very small step away from your dog, but at the same time provide distractions for your dog e.g., rustle paper or keys or if indoors ask someone to open or shut a door.
4 Return to the dog's side after ten seconds.
5 Praise release and play.

At stage 3, if necessary, carry out correction as previously described.

Twelfth Exercise

1 With the dog on the lead place him sitting in the Heel position.
2 Give the command 'Sit'.
3 Take a very small step away from your dog, but this time provide the greatest distraction, i.e. ask someone to call your dog's name.

The Sit Stay

Continue to repeat the tenth exercise until the dog remains stable whilst the lead is gently pulled from any direction.

4 Return to your dog's side after ten seconds.
5 Praise release and play.

Again at stage 3 if necessary carry out correction as previously described.

Increase the time that your dog is left sitting until he can remain in situ for one minute.

When you have achieved this return to Exercise 7 but drop the lead over the dog's shoulder. Proceed at a pace suitable to your dog through exercises 7 to 12 with the lead dropped over the dog's shoulder.

If your dog moves his position, quickly take up the lead and correct.

Praise the dog once he is in the Sit.

Release and play, then re-commence the exercise.

When the dog remains sitting with the lead over his shoulder whilst you walk round him and in spite of all distractions, he is ready to be left.

Thirteenth Exercise

1 Have the dog on the lead sitting in the Heel position.
2 Give the command 'Sit'.
3 Walk away from the dog counting to three.
4 Return to the dog's side and pick up the lead.
5 Praise release and play.

The Sit Stay

Gradually increase the time away from your dog until he can be left for one minute. Position yourself so that you can see any movement your dog makes and immediately correct it.

When your dog will remain in a Sit Stay for three minutes you can commence leaving your dog and going out of sight.

Fourteenth Exercise

At first teach this exercise in a familiar room.

1 Have your dog sitting in the Heel position facing the door, with the lead on.
2 Give the command 'Sit'.
3 Place the lead over the dog's shoulders.
4 Leave your dog and walk out of the door until just out of sight and return immediately to the Heel position.
5 Praise release and play.

Should the dog move, return, replace him in the correct position, then praise and release and start again.

Slowly increase the time that you are out of your dog's sight until you can leave him for one minute.

Fifteenth Exercise

Have your dog in a familiar room.

1 Have your dog sitting with the lead on facing the door.
2 Give the command 'Sit'.
3 Place the lead over the dog's shoulders.
4 Leave your dog, go through the door and close it. Immediately open the door again and return to the dog's side.
5 Praise and release.

Frequently the dog will move as the door closes. This is why you should return immediately. If there has been any movement, correct, praise and release and then repeat the exercise.

Never attempt out of sight Stays in strange surroundings until the dog is reliable on home ground. Once he is confident at home then he can be taken out to a park with all its distractions. When this is attempted you must start with exercise 14. Trees, bushes, cars, gates etc. can be utilised to enable the handler to go out of sight, but walk behind them and immediately return to your dog, coming back in the same direction as you went.

When your dog is happy to remain sitting for several minutes whilst you are out of sight then you can proceed to teach the Down Stay followed by the Stand Stay.

With each new position return to exercise 1 and work through as for the Sit Stay. The speed at which you progress through the exercises will depend on your dog's ability and confidence and only you, the handler, can decide this.

Obviously if the Sit Stay has been thoroughly taught the various stages can be gone through quickly for the other positions.

They should *not*, however, be omitted.

When teaching heelwork, to carry out the basic movement to teach the command 'Close' and the exercises for the left turns the lead is held in the *right hand.*

To guide the dog back, the left hand slides down the lead with the palm open and facing backwards.

To bring the dog forwards the wrist is twisted so that the palm faces forwards.

3

Heelwork

The regulations for heel-work laid down by the Kennel Club in January 1985 are as follows.

Heel on Lead. *'The dog should be sitting straight at the handler's side. On command the handler should walk briskly forward in a straight line with the dog at heel. The dog should be approximately level with and reasonably close to the handler's leg at all times when the handler is walking. The lead must be slack at all times. On the command "Left Turn" or "Right Turn" the handler should turn smartly at the right angle in the appropriate direction and the dog should keep its position at the handler's side. Unless otherwise directed, at the command "About Turn" the handler should turn about smartly on the spot through an angle of 180 degrees to the right and walk in the opposite direction, the dog maintaining its position at the handler's side. On the command "Halt" the handler should halt immediately and the dog should sit straight at the handler's side. Throughout this test the handler may not touch the dog or make use of the lead without penalty.'*

Heel Free. *'This test should be carried out in a similar manner as for Heel on Lead except that the dog must be off the lead throughout the test.'*

By courtesy of the Kennel Club.

Heelwork must be taught stage by stage just like any other exercise. Imagine what it would be like if you had no understanding of what was required of you and someone placed a slip chain around your neck, attached it to a lead and walked off dragging you with them; making left turns and right turns, yanking on the chain at every turn. I am sure you would agree that there must be a better way.

The art of good heelwork is to teach the dog to initiate movements with his hind-quarters as well as his fore-quarters, instead of his rear always simply following his front.

There is one command only for heelwork. I use the word *CLOSE* because it is not as flat and depressing as the word *heel* and can be intoned in a variety of ways.

The command 'Close' means get close to my left leg and remain there until given another command or released; move with my left leg and sit if my left leg becomes stationary. Dispense with all other commands such as 'get back', 'get in'. *Do not* use the command 'Sit' because if you tell your dog to sit and he does, then you must praise him. If he sits but is crooked, then you are praising him for being incorrectly placed. If you correct him then you are at fault for he has done what you said. You may argue that you can give the command 'Sit Close' but a quick responsive dog will sit on the 'Ss' sound. If, when your dog is working without commands, he fails to sit on a halt, the command you will give is 'Close' whilst you place him in the 'Sit'.

Whilst teaching all the following movements endeavour to keep the dog's head up so that you have his full attention, and make sure that all his 'Sits' are straight. Before attempting any exercise be certain that you are sure of the movements required so that *YOU* will move smoothly and confidently.

Although I have had to describe all the exercises in succession, they should be taught one at a time, and you should not teach the next stage until the preceding one is thoroughly learnt. This may take days, weeks or months according to the abilities of you and your dog.

The first stage of teaching heelwork is to teach the young dog to move into the heel position on being given the command 'Close'.

Heelwork

The Basic Movement to teach the command 'Close'

1 Have your dog on the lead sitting by your side in the heel position and the lead in your *right hand.*

2 Give the command 'Sit' and take one step to the right.

3 Give your dog's name for attention, followed by the command 'Close'. →

5 Praise release and play.

Stage 3 shown from behind.

→

At the same time take your left leg straight back behind your body and slide the left hand down the lead (as described) guiding the dog back in an arc until he is level with, and parallel to, your left leg. Close your left leg to your right leg bringing the dog forward with your left hand (as described).

4 When your left leg is still, place the dog in the Sit position repeating the command 'Close'.

Repeat this Basic movement five or six times in succession at each training session until the dog moves voluntarily and requires very little help to get into the Heel position. When this has been accomplished proceed to teach the following exercises. Once the dog understands the command 'Close' you can vary your training by sometimes carrying out the figure of eight as described under 'Heelwork on the Move'. Never do this at this level without using the dog's toy.

Notes

Heelwork

First Exercise Teaching the Left and

1 These turns require the dog to move his hind-quarters backwards whilst barely moving his front legs. Have the dog sitting in the heel position and the lead in the right hand. Give the command 'Sit'.

2 Leave your dog and walk forwards to the end of the lead, left turn and halt. →

Close your left leg to your right leg bringing the dog forward with your left hand.

4 When your left leg is still, place the dog in the Sit position repeating the command 'Close'. →

Left About Turns

3 Give the dog's name and the command 'Close'. At the same time take your left leg straight back behind your body,

and slide the left hand down the lead guiding the dog back in an arc until he is level with, and parallel to, your left leg.

5 Praise release and play.

Notes

Repeat this exercise until the dog moves confidently. Gradually make the movement tighter by decreasing the distance between yourself and your dog until you take a small step forward and a left turn.

Heelwork

Second Exercise

1 Have the dog sitting in the heel position with the lead in the right hand Give the command 'Sit', taking a step to the right.

2 Give the dog's name followed by the command 'Close'. At the

same time take your left l
straight back directly
behind your body and slic

at the same time taking the left leg back

guiding the dog back with your left hand as though he was attached to your leg.

Close your left leg to you
right leg keeping the dog

the left hand down the lead guiding the dog back in an arc until he is level with, and

parallel to, your left leg. Close your left leg to your right leg bringing your dog forward with your left hand,

but continue the movement by pivoting on the right leg making a quarter turn to the left,

position and halt placing

the dog in the 'sit' position.

Notes

3 Praise release and play.

Heelwork

Third Exercise

1 Have the dog sitting in the heel position and the lead in the right hand.
2 Give the command 'Sit'.
3 Make a left turn so that you are facing his left shoulder.
4 Give the dog's name followed by the command 'Close'. At the same time take the left leg back and guide the dog with the left hand so that he moves his hind-quarters smoothly back making the minimum movement necessary with his fore-quarters until he is parallel to your left leg.
5 Close your left leg to your right leg bringing the dog into the Sit at the heel position.
6 Praise release and play.

This should never be attempted until the dog is very confident and experienced.

Fourth Exercise

1 Have the dog sitting in the heel position and the lead in the right hand.

2 Give the dog's name and the command 'Close'. →

3 When he has successfully moved

his hind-quarters backwards so that he is

parallel to the left leg, halt with both legs together

placing the dog in the Sit position. →

Pivot on the right leg in an anti-clockwise direction with the left leg a little behind the right leg.

Guide the dog with the left hand on the lead

so that he moves backwards

in a left-about movement.

4 Praise release and play.

Notes

Fifth Exercise

1 Have the dog sitting in the heel position and the lead in the right hand.
2 Give the dog's name and the command 'Close'. Pivot on the right leg in an anti-clockwise direction with the left leg a little behind the right leg. Guide the dog with the left hand on the lead so that he moves backwards in a left-about movement. When he has successfully moved his hind-quarters backwards so that he is parallel to the left leg, take a step forward after completing the turn and then release and play.

When your dog has learnt to move his hind-quarters back easily proceed to teach the right turns.

Heelwork

First Exercise Teaching the Right and Right

If your dog truly understands the command 'Close' and has mastered the left turn; and if your have kept your dog happy by playing vigorously between each exercise, the right turns should come easily.

The following exercises all start with the Basic Movement, as before, but the lead is held in the *left hand*. Before you go into the turn bring your right hand across the front of your body and lightly grasp the lead, guiding your dog onto your left leg and bringing him round with you.

1 Have the dog sitting in the Heel position with the lead in your *Left hand*. Give the command 'Sit'. Leave your dog by taking a step to the right. →

hand until he is level with and parallel to your left leg.

3 Close your left leg to your right leg

and finish with the dog sitting in the Heel position. →

about Turns

2 Give the dog's name followed by the command 'Close'. At the same time take your left leg straight back behind your body guiding the dog back in an arc with the left

4 Praise release and play.

Notes

Once you and your dog are making this movement smoothly with the lead in the left hand, proceed with the following exercises:

Heelwork

Second Exercise

1 Have the dog sitting in the Heel position with the lead in your left hand. Give the command 'Sit'.

2 Leave your dog and take one step to the right and one step forward. →

Repeat the command 'Close' and pivot, making a *Right Turn* using your right hand on the lead to guide the

dog onto your left leg and bringing him round with you. →

3 Give the dog's name and the command 'Close'. At the same time take your left leg straight back behind your body guiding the dog with the left hand until he is level with and parallel to your left leg. As your left leg closes to your right leg bring your right hand across the front of your body and lightly grasp the lead.

Halt with your dog sitting in the Heel position.

4 Praise release and play.

Notes

Heelwork

Third Exercise

1 Have the dog sitting in the Heel position with the lead in your left hand. Give the command 'Sit'.

2 Leave your dog and take one step to the right and one step forward. →

Repeat the command 'Close'

and pivot into a *Right About Movement*,

using your right hand on the lead →

3 Give the dog's name and the command 'Close'. At the same time take your left leg straight back behind your body guiding the dog back

with the left hand until he is level with and parallel to your left leg.

As your left leg closes to your right leg bring your right hand across the front of your body and lightly grasp the lead.

to guide the dog round with your left leg.

4 Take a step forward after completing the turn and then release and play.

Points to Remember

1 Once the dog has mastered all these movements, gradually increase the level of difficulty by combining two or three before releasing.
2 Always start with the Basic Movement, moving the left leg back. This will serve the purpose, when effecting the right turn and right about turn, of teaching the dog to come in to and out of the turns with his back end straight.
3 Always give the command 'Close' preceded by the dog's name to get his attention.
4 Always praise when the dog is in the correct position.
5 Always release with *Vigorous* play to prevent boredom.

Heelwork

Teaching Heelwork on the Move

When you are sure that your dog understands the word 'Close' and knows how you wish him to negotiate the turns, it is time to teach him heelwork. First you must test his readiness.

Have your dog on the lead playing with his carpet/toy. Use your voice to get him excited, e.g., say in an excited way, 'Let's go; Are you going to do heelwork?' etc. Then say his name for attention and give the command 'Close' and walk a few paces in a straight line. If he voluntarily gets into the heel position and comes with you, give profuse praise and release and play.

He is now ready to do heelwork. If he does not get into the heel position and go with you he is not ready, so spend more time on the previous exercises. He may just need a few more days of these.

With the dog on the lead and playing with his carpet/toy, get him excited and tell him he is going to do heelwork.

Give the dog's name followed by the command 'Close' and move off into a left hand circle progressing into a figure of eight. Keep the lead in your left hand and your dog's toy in your right hand, all the time giving plenty of verbal praise and encouragement. At first keep moving for only a few seconds before throwing the carpet/toy and releasing your dog. When executing a figure of eight use your right hand to draw your dog forward should he hang back when he is on the outside and check him back gently should he surge forward when he is on the inside. Keep the movements of the lead firm but short and every time the lead is used repeat the command 'Close'. Immediately after each correction praise your dog. Use your voice and the carpet/toy to keep your dog happy and keen. GRADUALLY build up the length of time that the dog is working, keeping control so that he neither surges forward nor hangs back. Step out confidently in a natural manner. Never wait for your dog, never look back at him, but when he is in the correct position look down at him with a pleased expression as this will give him confidence. Occasionally work at a semi-fast pace; never let him get bored. Give praise when the dog is in the correct position and release by letting him play with his carpet/toy.

Once your dog is happily keeping on your left leg, whilst you execute a figure of eight, the time has come to teach more formal heelwork.

1 Have your dog on the lead, relaxed and happy, playing with his carpet/toy. Tell him he is going to do heelwork.
2 Give his name followed by the command 'Close' and walk off into a figure of eight. When you are collected and ready turn into a straight line for a few paces, make a left turn and halt, making sure that your dog sits straight.
3 Praise, release and play.

Repeat this, first ending with a right turn, then a right about turn, then a left about turn; always keeping the 'want' by making it exciting and releasing with play.

Gradually increase the number of paces taken after the turn before halting. Intersperse straight heelwork with a figure of eight. When you feel that your dog is ready, increase the number of turns before halting.

When you are getting good response without any aid except your voice and the carpet, try formal heelwork commencing with the dog sitting in the heel position.

Points to Remember

1 Always train on the lead and use your lead the second that your dog moves position.
2 Start with the dog playing and excited and go into a figure of eight before walking in a straight line. Only occasionally start with the dog sitting in the heel position.
3 Give plenty of verbal encouragement but do not be so monotonous that your words of praise cease to have any meaning; neither be so extravagant with your words of praise that you have nothing extra to give when your dog has done something really worth praising.
4 Always make sure that your dog sits when you halt and that the Sits are straight. Remember to give the command 'Close' and not 'Sit'.
5 Use the piece of carpet to release your dog with and as an aid to keep his attention.
6 Always repeat the command 'Close' if any correction is given and immediately follow with praise.
7 If the dog does not execute a turn correctly take him back and execute the appropriate exercise used to teach that particular turn.
8 If you lose your dog's attention, execute a turn smartly, correcting with the lead and repeating the command 'Close', immediately praise and then release.
9 Make sure that the dog is in the correct position at the time that you praise and release by throwing the carpet.
10 Remember that a few seconds of good heelwork followed by a game is better than minutes of indifferent heelwork.
11 NEVER stop training the 'on the spot' heelwork exercises using the basic movement.

4

Deportment and Footwork

I am not going to attempt to write down instructions on footwork. Firstly because I, like so many others, have spent hours trying to learn perfect footwork only to find that as soon as I am working with my dog it all goes haywire and is therefore a complete waste of time. Secondly, the Kennel Club rules state that heelwork should be carried out in a happy natural manner, and I do not think that careful clockwork placing of the feet when turning can honestly be classed as that.

However, I do believe that how you walk and turn assists your dog to maintain the correct position by your side, therefore deportment is important. The two important aspects of walking in the ring are your balance, which will give you smoothness and is determined by having your body upright but not rigid, and walking in a straight line. Both of these are aided by your eyes. For example, if you were walking down the road and someone called you from behind or from the side, you would hear first, then your eyes and head would turn towards the sound and your body would follow. You would not think to yourself 'Am I on the correct foot for turning?' or 'Where should the next foot be placed?' etc. In fact your body would follow your eyes and at no time would you consider your feet.

It is on that principle that I base my footwork. I suggest that you walk in a straight line and at some point decide to turn right. Look in that direction and take notice of what happens to your feet. Most of you will find that you will pivot on the right foot, balance yourself with a very small step with the left foot and walk out of the turn with the right foot. If you decide to turn left I think that you will find that after your eyes and head have turned you will pivot on the left foot, take a small balancing step with the right foot, and walk out of the turn with the left foot. The Right-about and Left-about turns are simply an extension of this. Some people will need to tidy up their natural turn in order not to leave their dog behind or push him away from their left leg.

The main thing to remember is that the closer together the feet are during a turn the easier it is for the dog to remain close. Therefore, keep your strides small and your knees in close proximity to each other when going into and out of a turn.

In the more advanced obedience classes the turning of your head and shoulders first could be construed as an extra command. However, by this time you should be sufficiently experienced to be able to use your eyes to negotiate the turns without ever extenuating the head and shoulder movement.

5

The 'Watch' Command

When the dog is given the command 'Watch' he should immediately give his whole attention to his handler. That means he must look at as well as listen to the person in control.

It is a useful command to use in any exercise when the dog has become distracted, particularly in exercises where the dog is at some distance from you. Although it should be taught early as an exercise you should only use it in training when the dog is experienced.

For example, when you are carrying out the Novice Recall exercises and your dog, although he has remained in the position in which you left him, is giving his attention to other things. Give the command 'Watch' in a very dominant way. This will bring the dog's mind back to you and to what he is doing without allowing him to move. The same thing would apply if your dog was in the down position waiting to be called to heel but his attention is elsewhere.

This exercise is taught initially in the Heel Position. It is very important to have the dog in the correct position, i.e., with his feet in line with your instep. If the dog is too far forward you will teach him to turn his shoulders and not just his head.

Correct position of hands when giving the command 'Watch'.

Incorrect position of hands when giving the command 'Watch'.

The Watch Command

First Exercise

1 With the dog in the correct heel position.

2 Place your right hand under his jaw and tilt his head upwards. Use your left hand to steady and caress the dog's head.

3 When eye to eye contact is made give the command 'Watch'. Slowly release pressure from the right hand and tickle the dog under his chin, and praise.

4 Praise release and play.
Repeat this exercise six times in succession.

Second Exercise

1 With the dog in the correct heel position.

2 Place your right hand under his jaw and tilt his head upwards. Use your left hand to steady and caress the dog's head.

3 When eye to eye contact is made give the command 'Watch'. Whilst the eye contact is being maintained remove the right hand from his jaw.

4 Praise, release and play.

The Watch Command

Third Exercise

1 With the dog in the correct heel position.

2 Place your right hand under his jaw and tilt his head upwards. Use your left hand to steady and caress the dog's head. →

5 If eye contact is maintained tickle the dog under his chin with the right hand and praise.

6 Release and play.

3 When eye to eye contact is made give the command 'Watch'. Whilst eye to eye contact is maintained remove the right hand from his jaw.

As this is a static exercise and could become boring for the dog ensure that the play is exciting and vigorous each time you repeat the exercise.

4 Remove the left hand from the side of his head.

Notes

The Watch Command

Fourth Exercise

1 With the dog in the correct heel position. Give the command 'Watch' once eye contact is made.

2 Swing the right hand across and gently touch the dog under his chin with your finger tips two or three times, at the same time.

3 Praise, e.g., 'Super Dog', 'That's Clever', etc. Release and play.

4 If your dog moves his head or eyes in any of these exercises before being released quickly return your hands to their position in Exercise 1, i.e. place your right hand under his jaw and tilt his head upwards and use your left hand to steady and caress his head, repeat the command and complete the exercise.

Do not progress to Exercise 5 until your dog makes immediate and voluntary eye contact with you on the command 'Watch'.

The Watch Command

Fifth Exercise

1 Have the dog on the lead and the lead in your left hand. Have your dog playing. Walk backwards keeping your dog just within arms' reach.

3 Swivel to the heel position keeping the dog's head up.

Whilst keeping his head up →

2 Use the dog's name in an excited way followed by the command 'Watch', at the same time tapping him under the chin with the right hand. Once the dog is pacing towards you making eye contact, praise.

move into the Sit position.

4 Praise release and play.

The Watch Command

Sixth Exercise

1 With the dog in the correct heel position.
2 Give the command 'Watch' once eye contact is made.
3 Whilst eye contact is being made have someone call your dog. Immediately the dog moves his head or eye quickly return your hands to their position in Exercise 1, i.e. place your right hand under his jaw and tilt his head upwards and use your left hand to steady and caress his head and repeat the command 'Watch'. Praise whilst eye contact is being maintained.
4 Release and play.

Seventh Exercise

This exercise should not be attempted unless your dog has a reliable controlled Sit. With the dog on the lead and sitting give the command 'Sit'. Go to the end of your lead and face your dog. Give the command 'Watch'. Have someone call him. If he moves his head or eyes immediately move towards him repeating the command 'Watch'. If he responds, praise and return to the heel position and release. If he does not respond return to the heel position and carry out Exercise 1.

Eighth Exercise

This exercise is for dogs who fully understand Heel Work and are quite advanced in their training. Have the dog on the lead doing heel work and with the lead in the left hand have someone distract him either by calling his name or in some other way. If the dog looks away give the command 'Watch', at the same time tighten up the lead with the left hand and swing the right hand across tapping the dog under his chin. Walk on a few paces. Release and play.

Remember

1 When making eye contact do not stare into the dog's eyes as this will be seen as a threat. Pick a point in between the eyes.
2 The tap under the chin must be done with the finger tips. It is not a *bang* under the chin with the flat of the hand. This exercise, if done correctly, can also help correct the dog who likes to push his head into the handler's body in the present position or the dog who hangs his head during heel work.
3 Speed of reaction is essential for good results.
4 Do not attempt to use the command at a distance until you are absolutely sure that the dog understands the command and differentiates it from all others.
5 When using distractions to enforce the command in heel work remember to tighten the lead in order to maintain the dog in the correct position.

Notes

The regulations for the Novice Recall as laid down by the Kennel Club in January 1985, are as follows:

'Recall from the sit or down position at handler's choice. Dog to be recalled by handler when stationary and facing the dog. Dog to return smartly to handler, sit in front, go to heel – all on command of judge or steward to handler. Distance at discretion of judge. Test commences when handler leaves the dog.'

By courtesy of the Kennel Club

6

The Novice Recall

The Novice Recall consists of four parts:

1 The controlled sit.
2 The return to the handler.
3 The present.
4 The finish.

The Return to the Handler.

This is the most important part of the novice recall. It is the first part to be taught and ideally the teaching starts when the dog is very young.

For example, when you are feeding a young dog, before you put his food on the floor say the dog's name followed by the command 'Come'. Say the word 'Come' in the tone you intend to use when the dog is at a distance even if the dog is very near you. Do the same if you are giving the dog titbits or vitamin tablets, etc. When you are out walking your dog call him occasionally and give a titbit. This will ensure that the dog has pleasant associations with the command 'Come'.

The Novice Recall

To Teach the Command 'Come'

1 Have the dog on the lead but doing his own thing. Call the dog's name to get his attention and follow with the command 'Come'. Move backwards *gently* reeling him in until he is right up close to you.

2 Have him jump up and play with you.

Repeat this several times at each session. Keep the dog happy and keen to come to you by playing with him immediately he reaches you. Use distractions in order to teach the dog that no matter what he is doing the command 'Come' must be obeyed.

Only use the commmand 'Come' if the dog is on the other end of the lead so that he always has to obey it. In the early stages the dog might resist on the end of the lead but once the command has been given make sure it is obeyed. Always Praise and Play even if the dog does not come willingly.

Do not progress until he responds to the command voluntarily.

Once the dog is coming to you fast without compulsion you can teach the Present.

The Novice Recall

The Basic Movement to Teach the Present

The Present

This cannot be taught until you have mastered the controlled 'Sit'. The command for the present is also 'Come', because the command means come and sit in front of me close enough for me to handle you in comfort.

Do not use the command 'Sit' in this exercise, as when learning the Distant Control the dog will have learnt to go backwards into the Sit position and this will cause him to sit too far away from you. Also, a well trained dog will sit immediately he hears the command.

Therefore should he be crooked when you give the command he will sit crooked. Thus you might easily teach your dog to sit back from you in a crooked fashion and then have the gall to correct him for doing what he has been told.

Notes

1 Have your dog on the lead. Sit comfortably in a chair. Draw the dog towards you with the lead. When he is

between your feet slip your hands, with the palms facing towards your body, into the

dog's collar under his chin. Ease the dog into the present position, i.e., sitting straight in

front of you and near to you at the same time giving the command 'Come Straight'.

2 Give the dog a reward and Praise. Release and play.

The Novice Recall

First Exercise

1 Have your dog on the lead and tell him he is going to do a recall. Give the command 'Sit'. (This the dog will know from both the Stay and Distant Control exercises). Stand in front of and facing the dog, step back to the end of the lead.

2 Give the dog's name followed by the command 'Come', at the same time extending the arms sideways; immediately return them to the body so that the hands meet in the centre of the body, at a level suitable to the size of the dog.

3 As soon as the dog is within easy reach, slip your hands into the dog's collar and draw him into the sit as described in the Basic Movement, i.e. by slipping your hands, with the palms facing towards your body, into the dog's collar under his chin.

4 Praise. Swivel into the heel position.

5 Praise release and play.

Notes

When the dog understands that the command 'Come' means return and sit in front of the handler, you can begin doing recalls from different angles.

Footnote

By swivel I mean take your weight on your left foot and turn backwards so that you return to the Heel Position. This means that the exercise ends with the dog in the Heel Position without him always carrying out a finish.

The Novice Recall

Second Exercise

1 With the dog sitting, stand in front of and facing him at the end of the lead. Take a step to the right. Call the dog in as before with the command 'Come'. At the same time put the left leg forward so that the dog has to go round →

Complete the Present as before with the Basic Movement. Praise.

2 Swivel to the heel position.

→

it before sitting in the present position. Use the lead to guide the dog round the leg, and return the leg next to the stationary leg as soon as the dog has gone round it.

3 Praise release and play.

The Novice Recall

Third Exercise

1 With the dog sitting, stand in front of and facing him at the end of the lead.
2 Take a step to the *left*.
3 Call the dog in as before with the command 'Come'. At the same time put the *right* leg forward so that the dog has to go round it before sitting in the Present position. Draw the leg back as the dog comes in.
4 Complete the Present as before with the Basic Movement. Praise.
5 Swivel to the heel position.
6 Praise release and play.

When teaching this exercise do not always demand a Present. Sometimes call the dog and let him jump up.

When a 'Present' is demanded bring the hands to the centre of the body. When a 'Present' is not demanded keep the arms outstretched.

Do not progress by giving the command 'Come' when the dog is free until you feel that he responds reliably. Test the dog's response occasionally when he is free but within arms' reach.

Give his name and the command 'Come'.

Use the hands as previously described and see if he completes the 'Return' and the 'Present' correctly.

Once the dog understands and responds to the command 'Come', proceed to teach the 'Finish'.

Points to Remember

1 The name is only for attention; the command is 'Come'.
2 Do not always ask for a 'Present'.
3 Do not follow the Recall with a 'Finish' in training.
4 Do not stop training Novice Recalls no matter what class you are working.
5 Frequently call from free running.

Notes

7

The Finish

The Kennel Club regulations simply state that the dog 'must go to heel'. Therefore the handler may choose how this is done. Most of the dogs taught heelwork by my method will naturally attempt the continental finish rather than the English method. However, before attempting this exercise I test the dog in order to see if he has any natural preference.

Have your dog in the sit position. Stand in front of him but close to his feet. Give the command 'Close'. Observe his reactions.

If the dog attempts to go backwards and to the left then proceed to teach the Continental Finish.

If the dog attempts to go round you via your right leg or sits and looks at you in an uncomprehending manner then teach the English Finish.

The Finish

First Exercise The Continental Finish

This, when executed correctly gives a lighter, cleaner finish and you are less likely to have such problems as inattention and slowness.

1 Have your dog sitting in front of you on the lead with the lead in your *right hand.* Move your left leg next to the dog's left side level with his *hind-quarters.* →

3 Close your left leg to your right leg placing the dog in the Sit position. →

2 Give the command 'Close' and at the same time move the left leg back and slide the left hand down the lead until it is near the dog's collar.

Take the dog back and bring his head round onto your left leg.

4 Praise release and play.

Second Exercise

1 Have your dog sitting in front of you on the lead with the lead in your *right hand*. Move your left leg next to the dog's left side level with his *shoulder*.

2 Give the command 'Close' and again at the same time move the left leg back and slide the left hand down the lead until it is near the dog's collar. Take the dog back and bring his head round onto your left leg and bring the dog forward with your left leg.

3 Close your left leg to your right leg placing the dog in the Sit position.

4 Praise release and play.

The Finish

Third Exercise

1 Have your dog sitting in front of you on the lead with the lead in your *right hand.* Remain in front of your dog but this time *do not* move your left leg to the dog's side.

2 Give the command 'Close' and again at the same time move the left leg back and slide →

3 Close your left leg to your right leg placing the dog in the Sit position. →

the left hand down the lead until it is near the dog's collar. Take the dog back and bring his

head round onto your left leg and bring your dog forward with your left leg.

4 Praise release and play.

Notes

The Finish

First Exercise The English Finish

1 Have the dog on the lead with the lead in your *left hand*. Stand close to, and facing the dog's right side.

2 Give the command 'Close'. Use your *right hand* on the lead to guide your →

and draw him into the heel position with the left hand.

3 Finish in the Sit position. →

dog round your right leg

4 Praise release and play.

Notes

The Finish

Second Exercise

1 Have the dog on the lead with the lead in your *left hand.* Stand close to the dog with your right leg next to the dog's right shoulder.

2 Give the command 'Close'. Use your *right hand* on the lead to guide your →

and draw him into the Heel position with the left hand.

3 Finish in the 'Sit' position. →

dog round your right leg

4 Praise release and play.

Notes

The Finish

Third Exercise

1 Have the dog on the lead. Stand in front of your dog with the lead in your *left hand.*

2 Give the command 'Close'. Use your *right hand* on the lead to guide →

drawing the dog into the Heel position with your *left hand.*

3 Finish in the Sit position. →

the dog round your right leg

4 Praise release and play.

Notes

Remember, the lead is held in the *right hand* and the left hand is used to guide the dog in the Continental Finish.

The lead is held in the *left hand* and the right hand is used to guide the dog in the English Finish.

This leads to the left or right arm signal used by most people as a command.

My method of opening the dog's mouth to receive the retrieve article.

The Kennel Club regulations as at January 1985 were as follows:

At the start of this exercise the dog should be sitting at the handler's side. On command the handler must throw the dumbell/article in the direction indicated. The dog should remain at the Sit position until the handler is ordered to send it to retrieve the dumbell/article. The dog should move out promptly at a smart pace to collect the dumbell/article cleanly. It should return with the dumbell/article at a smart pace and sit straight in front of the handler. On command the handler should take the dumbell/article from the dog. On further command the dog should be sent to heel. In classes A, B and C the test commences on the order 'last command' to handler.

By courtesy of the Kennel Club.

8

The Retrieve

The Retrieve consists of:

1 The Controlled Sit.
2 The Retrieve a Going out.
b Picking up.
c Returning.
3 The Present.
4 The Finish.

In this chapter I shall only deal with Part 2, i.e., the Retrieve, as the other components of the exercise have already been learnt as the Novice Recall.

I am often asked when to start teaching this exercise. I usually start about five-and-a-half months when the dog has cut his canine teeth. With a big dog I certainly would not leave it any later as the size of the dog may make it difficult to control him.

I always use a soft article to teach a puppy to retrieve, because a hard article such as a dumbell may not be easily accepted by a puppy. I find that the inside of a toilet roll stuffed with paper or a stocking stuffed is ideal.

The Retrieve

First Exercise To Reinforce the Controlled Sit

In the following exercises the illustrations are at different angles to show the positions of the hands and the feet more clearly.

1 Have the dog on the lead and sitting in the heel position. Kneel on the floor so that you are on a level with your dog. Tell the dog he is going to 'Retrieve'. Put the lead over your shoulder and hold the dog's collar

lightly with your left hand. Give the command 'Sit'. Drop the Retrieve article on the floor in front of the dog. If he attempts to investigate the article immediately prevent him and reinforce the 'Sit'.

2 Praise release and play and encourage the dog then to play with the article.

Continue to practise this exercise until your dog makes no attempt to move from the Sit position until released. It is pointless continuing until you have total control.

The Retrieve

Second Exercise

1 Have the dog on the lead and sitting in the heel position. Kneel on the floor so that you are on a level with your dog. Place the lead over your shoulder so that it is out of the way. Tell the dog he is going to 'Retrieve'. Place the three central fingers of the left hand (with the palm facing downwards) under the dog's collar. Place the article on the floor in front of the dog. →

3 As the article reaches the dog's mouth, slip the index finger of the right hand behind the dog's left canines and gently lever the mouth open.

4 Roll the article into the dog's mouth at the same time giving the command 'Hold'. →

2 Scoop the article up with the right hand, bringing it up towards the dog's mouth. Whilst doing this the left hand should control the dog's head, keeping it facing towards the article, thus facilitating the slipping of the article into the dog's mouth.

5 Immediately take the article and praise release and play with the article.

Continue to train this exercise until the dog voluntarily opens his mouth on the command 'Hold'. *N.B.* Never give the command 'Hold' until the article is actually entering the mouth.

Sometimes alternate Exercises 1 and 2 in order to maintain control.

The Retrieve

Third Exercise

1 Kneel on the floor so that you are on a level with your dog. Place the lead over your shoulder. Tell the dog that he is going to 'Retrieve'. Place the article on the floor in front of the dog.

2 As before scoop the article up with the right hand, bringing it up towards the dog's mouth. Whilst doing this the left hand should control the dog's head, keeping it facing towards the article, thus facilitating the slipping of the article into the dog's mouth. →

5 Gently guide the dog round into the Present position with the right hand on the collar under the chin and the left hand on the dog's right side giving the command 'Come'. →

3 As the article reaches the dog's mouth, again slip the index finger of the right hand behind the dog's left canines and gently lever the mouth open.

4 Roll the article into the mouth at the same time giving the command 'Hold'. Praise.

Take the article.

6 Praise release and play with the article.

The Retrieve

Fourth Exercise

1 Kneel on the floor so that you are on a level with your dog, place the lead over your shoulder, tell the dog that he is going to 'retrieve'. Place the article on the floor in front of the dog.

2 As before scoop the article up with the right hand, bringing it up towards the dog's mouth, at the same time push the dog's head down towards the article. →

collar under the chin and the left hand on the dog's right side giving the command 'Come'.

5 Take the article. →

3 Slip the article into the dog's mouth giving the command 'Hold'.

4 Gently guide the dog round into the Present position with the right hand on the

6 Praise release and play with the article.

Notes

Continue with this exercise until the right hand is not actually scooping the article off the floor. When exercise 4 can be carried out without the handler giving any physical compulsion proceed to teach the Retrieve standing upright instead of kneeling.

The Retrieve

Fifth Exercise Handler standing upright instead

Remember the illustration are at different angles.

1 Stand with your dog on the lead and the lead in the *left hand.* Have the dog sitting in the heel position. Give the command 'Sit'. Place the article one stride in front of you, at the same time exciting the dog by using your voice saying, for example, 'Are you going to Retrieve?, Are you ready?', etc. →

and with the *right hand* scoop the article into the dog's mouth. →

# of kneeling

2 Give the command 'Hold'. As the dog moves towards the article place your right leg across and forwards so that your foot is between the article and your dog.

3 Take the dog round your foot

4 Stand back in your original position and bring the dog into the Present with the command 'Come'. Take the article.

5 Praise release and play with the article.

The Retrieve

Sixth Exercise

Remember the illustrations are at different angles.

1 Stand with your dog on the lead and the lead in your *left hand.* Have the dog sitting in the heel position. Give the command 'Sit'. Place the article one stride in front of you, at the same time exciting the dog again by using your voice saying, for example, 'Are you going to Retrieve?, Are you ready?', etc. →

and allow him to pick up the article. →

2 Give the command 'Hold'. As the dog moves towards the article place your right leg across and forwards so that your foot is between the article and your dog.

3 Guide the dog round your foot

4 Stand back in your original position and bring the dog into the Present with the command 'Come'. Take the article.

5 Praise release and play with the article.

The Retrieve

Seventh Exercise

1 Have the dog on the lead and the lead in the *left hand*. Have the dog in the heel position. Give the command 'Sit'. Say the word Retrieve and place the article three paces in front of your dog. →

3 Give the command 'Hold'. As the dog moves towards the article place your right foot to the far side of it so that the dog goes behind the article before picking it up.

4 Turn and walk backwards to your original position, giving the command 'Come' and →

2 Take one pace back and stand sideways on to the article.

bringing the dog into the Present. Take the article.

5 Praise release and play with the article.

The Retrieve

Eighth Exercise

1 Have the dog on the lead and sitting in the Heel position. Give the command 'Sit'. Say the word Retrieve. Throw the article a short distance in front. →

3 Guide him into the Present position by using the lead and giving the command 'Come'.

4 Take the article. →

2 Give the command 'Hold' and allow the dog to retrieve it.

Notes

5 Praise release and play.

Ninth Exercise

As for exercise 8 but using a variety of articles. If the dog baulks at holding any particular article return to exercise 4 using the rejected article. *Do not use difficult articles in early stages.*

The Retrieve

Tenth Exercise To Enforce Total Control

1 Have the dog on the lead sitting in the Heel position. Give the command 'Sit'. Remove the lead. Throw out the article a short distance.

2 Walk out and collect the article and

walk back to your dog.

3 Praise the dog. Release and play.

The Retrieve

Eleventh Exercise

1 Have the dog on the lead sitting in the Heel position. Give the command 'Sit'. Remove the lead. Throw out the article a short distance.

2 Give the command 'Hold' and allow the dog to go out and retrieve. As soon as the article is in the dog's mouth give the command 'Come'.

3 Praise release and play.

Notes

The Retrieve

Points to Remember

1 Alternate these different exercises but initially do not proceed from one to the next unless the dog is carrying out the earlier one without contention.
2 Do not throw hard articles onto hard surfaces because initially the noise may worry or excite the dog. If the situation is unavoidable, place the article instead of throwing it.
3 Use the minimum of commands. As the dog picks up the article, very quietly say, 'Good dog, that's clever'.
4 When the dog is returning only use the voice if absolutely necessary.
5 Once you have given the command 'Hold' you must have a Present. When you are playing with the article tell the dog to 'Kill it' or 'Fetch'.
6 In order to prevent the dog releasing the article as soon as your arms move, sometimes move your arms or hands and at the same time repeat the command 'Hold' before taking the article. Sometimes swivel to the Heel position and take the article with the right hand.

If this procedure is followed slowly and methodically then mouthing should not occur. Mouthing is usually due to handlers shouting, getting excited, slapping the dog under the chin and throwing out too early and too far.

Dumbells

If you are competing, a dumbell is necessary for the Novice and 'A' Classes. The size is important and most people have them far too large. The dumbell should fit comfortably into the dog's mouth just behind the canine teeth. The sides should only just clear the dog's muzzle, but care must be taken that the ends do not press uncomfortably into the dog's cheeks.

Notes

The regulations for the 'A' Recall as laid down by the Kennel Club in January 1985 are as follows:

Recall from the Sit or Down position at handler's choice. Dog to be recalled to heel by handler, on command of judge or steward, whilst handler is walking away from dog, both to continue forward until halted. The recall and halt points to be the same for each dog and handler. Test commences following handler's last command to dog.

By courtesy of the Kennel Club.

9

The 'A' Recall

The 'A' Recall leads to the call-up from the box after the Sendaway; therefore I always teach it from the Down position. My aim is to get the dog from the Down position to the heel position as fast and as accurately as possible. This is the only exercise I teach off the lead. I combine the Novice Recall and the command Close, both of which the dog has already learnt. Teaching it this way gives the dog speed and enables the handler to use an arm signal from the start.

The 'A' Recall

First Exercise

1 Tell the dog you are going to do an 'A' Recall. Put the dog into the Down position. Give the command 'Down'. Leave the dog and walk in a straight line away from the dog for about eight paces. About turn and walk five paces towards the dog. Give the dog's name, at the same time extending both arms. →

3 As the dog reaches you, right turn, at the same time giving the command 'Close'.

If necessary talk the dog into the Heel position. →

2 As the dog responds give praise and encouragement in a very excited manner.

4 As soon as the dog is in the Heel position, Praise release and play.

Notes

It is important that the praise comes as soon as the dog has obeyed the command Close. Therefore, DO NOT continue to do heelwork but praise and release as soon as the dog is in the Heel position.

When the dog does not need praise and encouragement after you have given his name and extended both arms, proceed to exercise 2.

The 'A' Recall

Exercises 2 to 7 are similar to exercise 1 but with variations of the number of paces taken and the turns so no illustrations are given.

Second Exercise

1 Tell the dog you are going to do an 'A' Recall.
2 Put the dog into the Down position.
3 Give the command 'Down'.
4 Leave the dog and walk in a straight line away from the dog for about eight paces.
5 About turn and walk two paces towards the dog.
6 Give the dog's name at the same time extending both arms. As the dog reaches you, right turn and give the command 'Close'.
7 As soon as the dog is in the Heel position Praise release and play.

Third Exercise

1 Tell the dog you are going to do an 'A' Recall.
2 Put the dog into the Down position.
3 Give the command 'Down'.
4 Leave the dog and walk five paces away from the dog in a straight line.
5 About turn, give the dog's name at the same time extending both arms. As the dog reaches you right turn and give the command 'Close'.
6 Praise release and play.

Fourth exercise

1 Tell the dog you are going to do an 'A' Recall.
2 Put the dog into the Down position.
3 Give the command 'Down'.
4 Leave the dog and walk away in a straight line for about five paces, left turn and take one pace.
5 Twist the body to face the dog and extend the arms, at the same time giving the dog's name followed by the command 'Close'.
6 When the dog is in the correct position, Praise release and play.

Fifth Exercise

1 Tell the dog you are going to do an 'A' Recall.
2 Put the dog into the Down position.
3 Give the command 'Down'.
4 Leave the dog and walk away in a straight line for about five paces, left turn and take one pace.
5 Extend the left arm to the side and slightly turn the head at the same time.
6 Give the command 'Close'.
7 Praise release and play when the dog is in the correct position.

Sixth Exercise

1 Tell the dog you are going to do an 'A' Recall.
2 Put the dog into the Down position.
3 Give the command 'Down'.
4 Leave the dog and walk away in a straight line for about five paces, left turn and take one pace.
5 Either extend the left arm or turn the head whilst giving the command 'Close'.
6 Praise release and play.

Seventh Exercise

1 Tell the dog you are going to do an 'A' Recall'.
2 Put the dog into the Down position.
3 Give the command 'Down'.
4 Leave the dog and walk away in a straight line for about five paces.
5 About turn, give the dog's name and extend both arms. Just before the dog reaches you, left turn, giving the command 'Close'. Twist your body and encourage the dog into the Heel position.
6 Praise release and play as soon as he is in the correct position.

The 'A' Recall

Eighth Exercise

1 Tell the dog you are going to do an 'A' Recall. Put the dog into the Down position. Give the command 'Down'. Leave your dog and walk away in a straight line for about ten paces. Give your dog's name at the same time twisting your body round to the left towards the dog and extend your arms. →

turn back to your original position bringing the dog into the Heel position.

Right turn on the spot

2 As the dog reaches you

bringing your dog into the Sit position.

3 Praise release and play.

Gradually increase the walking before calling your dog and vary the pattern of your walking. Sometimes leave at the fast pace, sometimes incorporate a few halts. Build up the exercise into a complete 'A' Recall with some heelwork after the call-up.

Never stop helping your dog to make contact with your left leg and always Praise when he is there.

Giving scent from a cloth.

10

Scent Discrimination

The Kennel Club's Regulations for tests for obedience classes as laid down in January 1985, are as follows:

A steward will place the scent article amongst up to a maximum of nine other articles all of which should be clearly visible to the dog. The dog should at this time be facing away from the articles. On command the handler should bring the dog to a point indicated, give the dog scent and stand upright before sending the dog to find and retrieve the appropriate article. The dog should find the article and complete the test as for the Retrieve test. In all tests, scent articles are to be placed at least two feet apart. Limiting the time allowed for this test is at the Judge's discretion.

Class A. Handler's scent on Judge's Article.
'In this test at least one other article must be scented by someone other than the handler and the decoy article(s) must be similar for each dog.'

Class B. Handler's Scent on article provided by the Judge.
'The article must not be given to the dog. All articles must be separate and similar.'

Class C. Judge's Scent on a piece of marked cloth.
'A decoy steward should not handle a cloth for a period longer than the Judge.'

By courtesy of the Kennel Club.

Scent Discrimination

Do not attempt to teach this exercise until the dog is Retrieving reliably because Scent Discrimination is really an extension of the Retrieve exercise. The dog is asked to identify and retrieve the article which smells of the scent which has just been given to him.

Puppies are naturally inquisitive and where a human child would use his eyes the puppy uses its nose.

When a puppy is born obviously the first thing he does is to breathe but the second thing he does is to use his sense of smell to find his mother's nipples. He will continue to use this sense constantly throughout his life. In this exercise, therefore, you are once more harnessing a natural form of behaviour. The exercise must be taught in such a way that the dog enjoys it and wants to do it, because there is no way that compulsion can be used. Because I know that we cannot comprehend the dog's abilities, I try to teach scent discrimination in as natural a way as possible.

Stage 1

Whilst out walking with your dog throw a hotly scented easy-to-retrieve article into the grass, allowing the dog to see where it lands. Encourage the dog to find and retrieve it in the following manner: Walk with the dog pretending to look for it yourself, saying in an excited voice 'Find it', 'Where is it?' or 'Seek' etc. Encourage the dog in the correct direction so that he finds it quickly. Immediately he has located it give plenty of excited praise. Then give the command 'Hold'. When the dog has picked up the article, praise him again. Take the article and play with it.

Repeat this each day during the dog's walk, using a different article each time.

When the dog is carrying out Stage 1 quickly and with keenness proceed to:

Stage 2

Drop an article without the dog knowing. Walk on a few paces then turn back and look for it in the same way as in stage 1.

At this point choose the phrase which comes most naturally to you and use it to encourage the dog. This phrase will become associated in the dog's mind with the exercise, giving him the clue that he is going to do scent. Remember therefore, to make this phrase pleasant to your dog.

As soon as the dog has located the article praise him excitedly. Give the command 'Hold'. Stand still and give your dog a chance to present. He should automatically present following the command 'Hold'. Praise profusely and take the article and play with it with your dog.

Notes

Stage 3

Leave your dog in the Sit position. Walk out, with your dog watching you, and drop the hotly scented article in the grass so that it is not visible.

Return to your dog's side. Excite him with your 'Clue' words previously used and at the same time cup your hand just in front and around the dog's nose thus giving him your scent.

Give the command 'Find'.

Personally, I give the command 'Hold' to send my dog for scent. Before sending him and whilst I am giving him scent I excite him with all my 'Clue' words, e.g. 'Where is it?', 'Find it', 'You're going to do scent' etc. This tells my dog that he has to discriminate and not do a simple retrieve. However, some dogs find the use of the word 'Hold' confusing, so I suggest that you use the command 'Find'.

Encourage the dog whilst he is seeking. As soon as he has the article in his mouth Praise profusely.

Give the command 'Come'. Insist on a present. I always ask my dogs to present in all scent training so that even if the dog has to work for a long time before finding the article he will automatically present, whereas after working for a long time, a dog who has not always presented may lose concentration and forget to present.

Take the article. Praise release and play with the article. Each time you repeat this stage hide the article in a different place, e.g., behind a tree or bush or in long grass or use a fir cone and drop it amongst others.

Stage 4

Find some articles which have been lying outside for some time, pots, pieces of wood or even rubbish in a park (beware of glass). Carry out stage 3, placing your hotly scented article amongst them.

When your dog happily carries out stage 4, progress to the more formal exercises.

When using articles for scent always place them out with tongs or use plastic gloves so that they are scent free.

It is imperative to clean the articles after each session.

Two ways you can do this are

1. Put the articles into a strong plastic bag or container with holes made in it, wash them thoroughly under the tap and hang out in the garden.
2. Put the articles into a colander, wash and leave outside to dry.

Scent Discrimination

First Exercise

1 Have a variety of about ten articles not touched by you in a large circle. (At first use univiting articles.)

2 Place your article somewhere in the circle. →

All the time your dog is working, pivot so that you are constantly facing him, and encouraging him in an excited voice.

5 When he locates the article give the command 'Hold' if necessary. →

3 Stand in the centre of the circle, with your back to your article, with your dog in the Heel position. Give your dog scent from a cupped hand at the same time saying your clue words.

4 Stand upright and give the command 'Find' sending your dog.

6 When the article is in his mouth give the command 'Come' and insist on a Present. Praise. Take the article.

7 Release and play with the article.

The reason I stand in the middle of a circle is so that the dog only has to take a few paces before he presents.

Scent Discrimination

Second Exercise

Once your dog is carrying out exercise 1 confidently, repeat, but using more attractive articles such as a ball or furry article or sock, plus an article similar to the one with your scent on.

Third Exercise

Proceed as for exercises 1 and 2 but stand outside the circle with your dog in the heel position, and start and finish the exercise from there.

Fourth Exercise

Proceed as for exercises 1 and 3 but have your article placed about two feet behind the other articles.

Gradually progress to various patterns, e.g., half a circle with your article to the left, half a circle with your article to the right, L shapes, T shapes, V shapes etc.

Points to Remember

1 Keep the excitement.
2 Use a different article each time but hotly scented.
3 Stay close to the articles so that the dog is almost immediately in the Present position.
4 Initially look with the dog. If he is not keen, find it yourself, darting upon it, saying 'I've got it' and tease him by not letting him get it.
5 Never say 'No'. If your dog picks up the incorrect article go quickly to the correct one and point to it, saying 'What's this?' 'I've found it'. Invariably he will drop what he has in his mouth and come and see what you have got. Then you can give the command 'Hold'.
6 Always use tongs or plastic gloves.
7 Always ensure you use scent free articles.

Notes

Test 'B' Scent

This should follow naturally if you have constantly used different articles when teaching your dog scent and, if from exercise 2 on, you have used one article similar to the one with your scent on.

For your first attempt at a 'B' scent, place the articles, which must be all the same, in a circle. Stand in the middle and proceed as for exercise 1.

Progress through exercises 1 to 4 according to your dog's ability and confidence.

When your dog is confidently carrying out a 'B' scent of various patterns, occasionally use cloths and give your scent from a cloth.

1

2

3

4

5

Scent Discrimination

Giving Scent from a Cloth

When giving scent from a cloth, simply hold the cloth loosely in front of and slightly round the dog's nose.

The cloth should not be held tightly over the nose or mouth as this will restrict the flow of air carrying the scent into the dog's nostrils and it will be frightening for the dog.

The dog like you is breathing regularly and will therefore breathe in any scent placed near his nose. There is no need to pummel his chest or stomach. I am sure this is only an expression of the handler's anxiety. If the dog is worried about the cloth being held over his nose, have a piece of food in the palm of your hand with the cloth over it. Hold the cloth gently in front of his nostrils and allow him to find the food. This will condition the dog to have pleasant associations with the cloth and should overcome his fears.

Test 'C' Scent

When first being sent to perform Test 'C' exercise, the dog probably goes out looking for the handler's scent. He cannot find it but comes across the scent he has just been given and is therefore interested in it. He receives the command 'Hold', picks up the required cloth and receives profuse praise. Thus he learns that he is looking for the scent which has just been given.

When introducing your dog to 'C' scent seek the co-operation of a friend whom the dog knows and likes.

1 Have this person put his or her scent onto two cloths.
2 Place one of these cloths on the floor between, but at least two feet away from, two clean cloths.
3 Stand near to these cloths.
4 Have your friend give the dog scent from the second scented cloth, whilst you at the same give your dog the 'clue' words.
5 Send the dog. Have your friend move away from you.
6 When the dog hesitates over the scented cloth, give the command 'Hold'.
7 Praise as soon as the correct cloth is in your dog's mouth.
8 Give the command 'Come'.
9 Praise and release, playing with the cloth.

When this exercise is carried out confidently repeat the exercise but give the scent to the dog yourself.

Gradually increase the number of cloths on the floor.

At any time you have problems with your dog failing 'C' scent, return to a 'B' scent at a level which the dog does confidently. Slowly work through the stages as though your dog was learning 'B' and 'C' scent for the first time.

Never scold the dog for picking up the incorrect cloth or article. If the dog genuinely thinks he has the correct cloth (for reasons which we cannot know) you will only confuse and worry him.

The dog who always caused me anxiety over scent was my first dog 'Jess'. I never felt that she was reliable. I firmly believe that this was because I worried her by trying to *teach* her to use her nose instead of showing her which of the articles I wanted her to bring in.

The Kennel Club Regulations for the Sendaway as laid down in January 1985 are as follows:

On command of Judge to Handler, dog to be sent away in any direction indicated by the Judge. After the dog has been dropped handler will call the dog to heel whilst walking where directed by Judge and both will continue forward. No obstacle to be placed in the path of the dog. Simultaneous command and signal is permitted but as soon as the dog leaves the handler the arm must be dropped.

By courtesy of the Kennel Club.

11

The Sendaway

The Sendaway is often said to be the most unnatural of all the exercises. I really disagree with this point of view because when dogs are hunting they obviously have to run out and chase. I channel this natural instinct to teach the Sendaway, using my piece of carpet as the prey.

The Sendaway test consists of the following parts:

1 The controlled 'Sit'.
2 The 'Look' straight.
3 The Going away.
4 The immediate 'Drop'.
5 The Recall.

The Sendaway

Before teaching this exercise your dog must respond immediately to the command 'Down'.

The Down

Your dog will have learnt this command when being taught distant control. For the Sendaway it is simply a matter of increasing the speed of the dog's response.

1 With the lead in your *right hand* have your dog on the lead playing with you and his carpet.

2 Encourage him to jump in the air by teasing him with his carpet. When the dog is off the ground give the command 'Down'.

3 At the same time drop the carpet on the floor and slide the left hand down the lead towards the collar

propelling the dog onto the floor in the Down position.

4 Praise release and play.

Notes

This exercise can be repeated several times in succession as it is very enjoyable for the dog.

The Sendaway

The 'Look Straight'

It is important that before being sent the dog looks straight ahead and fixes his gaze forwards.

Place your piece of carpet on a chair.

Have your dog on a fairly short lead and walk him past the chair. As you pass it pick up the piece of carpet and throw it on the ground a little way in front of you, at the same time giving the command 'Look'. Run with the dog towards the carpet and pick it up without allowing the dog to get hold of it.

Tease the dog with the carpet. Finish by playing with the dog with the carpet.

Repeat this procedure at each training session until the dog fixes his gaze on the carpet and is really keen to get to the carpet. Do not progress until the dog responds correctly to the command 'Look'.

Notes

The Sendaway

First Exercise

Have your dog on a lead and the lead in your *left hand.* Have the piece of carpet in your *right hand.*

Get the dog excited by teasing him with the carpet and by telling him he is going to do Sendaways in an excited voice.

Keeping the lead in your left hand and the carpet in your right hand, move round in a tight circle two or three times, holding the carpet just in front of the dog's nose (but keeping it just out of reach), at the same time saying 'Sendaway' 'Look' 'Look' in a very excited voice. After circling two or three times and keeping the momentum throw the carpet out a short distance. Give the command 'Away' and run the dog out to the carpet.

Give the command 'Down' and drop the dog onto the carpet. Pat the carpet and praise the dog.

Release the dog and let him play with the carpet as though killing it.

Repeat this exercise several times in succession.

Do not progress until the dog is 'mad keen' to reach the carpet.

Second Exercise

Proceed as for the previous exercise up to the throwing out of the carpet but this time throw it out a greater distance. Again give the command 'Away' but this time let go the lead allowing the dog to go.

Follow up behind the dog very quietly. Give the command 'Down', dropping the dog on the carpet.

Immediately praise release and play.

Notes

The Sendaway

Third Exercise

1 Have the dog off the lead and sitting. Tell the dog he is going to do Sendaways. Leave the dog at point 'A' and run out at least 15 yards. Place the carpet on the floor at point 'B'. Kneel down so that you are sideways on to the carpet. Bang the carpet saying 'Look' 'Look'. →

and give the command 'Down'

dropping the dog onto the carpet. →

2 Give the command 'Away'. As the dog reaches you

twist him to face the way he has come

Notes

3 Praise release and play.

The Sendaway

Fourth Exercise

Repeat exercise 3 again but this time, after releasing and playing with your dog, drop the carpet on the floor i.e. at point 'B'.

Hold the dog lightly by the collar and run him back to his original starting place i.e. point 'A'. Get him excited but continue to restrain him lightly.

Give the command 'Look' followed by the command 'Away' and let him go. When the dog has covered about one third of the distance start to follow him.

Drop the dog on the carpet with the command 'Down'. Praise release and play.

At this point if your dog is not going out keenly it means that you have progressed too soon from one exercise to the next. On no account should you proceed any further unless your dog is going out fast and dropping immediately.

Notes

Fifth Exercise

Repeat exercise 3 again but this time, after releasing and playing with your dog, surreptitiously put the carpet in an easily accessible pocket. Keeping the dog excited and keen run him back to the original starting point 'A'.

Place him in the Sit and point him in the direction from whence he has come i.e. point 'B'.

Give the command 'Look' 'Look' keeping the excitement. Follow with the command 'Away' and allow the dog to go.

As the dog goes drop the carpet onto the floor behind you, i.e. at point 'A', and then quickly but quietly follow your dog.

With the command 'Down' drop your dog at point 'B'. Praise with a good deal of fuss.

Very quickly and keeping the excitement going Sit the dog at point 'B' and point him towards point 'A' giving the command 'Look'.

Follow with the command 'Away' and allow the dog to go back to the carpet at point 'A'.

Drop the dog on the carpet with the command 'Down'. Praise release and play with the carpet.

Notes

If the dog fails to obey the 'Away' command or stops half way, gently take him by the collar saying 'Sendaway' and run him to the carpet repeating the command 'Away'. Drop him on the carpet and praise profusely. Return to exercises 4 and 5 for a little while longer.

Repeat exercises 4 and 5 at your training sessions in various combinations, increasing the distance and varying the direction until your dog is going on command reliably and fast.

The Sendaway

Sixth Exercise   Introducing Boxes

1 Place a box around point 'B'. Leave your dog sitting in the box. *Run* and place the carpet at point 'A'. *Run* back to your dog.

2 Excite him, tell him is going to do 'Sendaways'. Give the command 'Look', pointing him towards the carpet.

3 Give the command 'Away' allowing the dog to go.

4 Follow up behind your dog.

5 Drop the dog down on the carpet giving the command 'Down'.

6 Praise release and play with the carpet.

As soon as the dog will sit in the box and totally ignore it proceed to Exercise 7.

The Sendaway

Seventh Exercise

1 This time leave your dog sitting at point 'A'. Run back to the box and place the carpet behind the box. Kneel sideways to the carpet. Pat the carpet giving your dog the command 'Away' 'Away' →

2 When your dog reaches you put him down with the command 'Down'. →

in a very excited voice.

3 Praise release and play.

Repeat exercise 6 and 7 using a variety of boxes. Do not proceed to exercise 8 until your dog totally ignores being in the boxes and going through them.

The Sendaway

Eighth Exercise

1 Leave your dog sitting in the box at point 'B'.
2 Run and place the carpet at point 'A'.
3 Kneel down sideways on to the carpet.
4 Pat the carpet giving the command 'Look'.
5 Give the command 'Away'.
6 Drop the dog onto the carpet with the command 'Down'.
7 Praise and fuss the dog.
8 Quickly sit the dog at point 'A'.
9 Run back through the box and place the carpet on the floor just behind the box.
10 Run back to your dog at point 'A'.
11 Give the command 'Look' making sure that the dog looks in the direction of the carpet.
12 Give the command 'Away'.
13 Follow up behind your dog.
14 Drop the dog on the carpet.
15 Praise release and play.

If your dog attempts to pick up any part of the box itself, quickly but calmly take the dog by the collar saying 'Sendaway' and run him to the carpet and drop him on it.

Praise release and play with the carpet.

Gradually progress until you can send your dog through the box and on to the carpet from any direction.

When you have achieved this place the carpet nearer and nearer to the box and finally proceed to exercise 9.

Notes

The Sendaway

Ninth Exercise

1 Leave your dog sitting at point 'A'. Run back to the box and place the carpet in the centre of the box. Run back to your dog. Give the command 'Away' allowing the dog to go.

2 Follow your dog and drop him on the carpet in the box.

After this occasionally send to nothing.

The Sendaway

Points to Remember

1 Speed is essential for a good straight Sendaway and Excitement is the key to obtaining and keeping the speed.
2 Because you are harnessing the dog's instinct to chase and kill you must have control of the Immediate Down. So always be firm about this and never allow your dog to 'Kill' the carpet before he has obeyed the command 'Down'. Should you be slow in giving the command 'Down' and thus allow the dog to take hold of the carpet before dropping, take it from him, place it back on the ground, and drop the dog on it.
3 Always be immediately behind your dog so that you can praise him on the spot as soon as he has dropped. For this reason make sure that you are full of energy before you embark on a training session.
4 Always send to a piece of carpet immediately you have sent to nothing.
5 Always release in the box during training, do not follow with the call-up.

The Recall from the Box

The call-up from the box is simply the 'A' Recall. You will already have taught this under the appropriate chapter.

Notes

The Regulations for heelwork in Class C as laid down by the Kennel Club in January 1985, are as follows:

The dog shall be required to work heel free, and also be tested at fast and slow pace. At some time during this test, at the discretion of the Judge, the dog shall be required, whilst walking to heel at normal pace, to be left at the Stand, Sit and Down in any order (the order to be the same for each dog) as and when directed by the Judge. The handler shall continue forward alone, without hesitation, and continue as directed by the Judge until he reaches his dog when both shall continue forward together until halted. Heelwork may include left about turns and figures of eight at normal and/or slow pace.

By courtesy of the Kennel Club.

12

Advanced Heelwork

Change of pace

Fast Heelwork

1 With your dog on the lead, get him excited by playing with his toy/carpet. Tell him that he is going to do heelwork.
2 Give the dog's name followed by the command 'Close' and walk off into a figure of eight, keeping your dog's attention with his toy.
3 When the dog is on the inside, and you are collected and ready, change smoothly into fast pace.
4 After a few paces slow down to normal.
5 Praise release and play.

When you have the dog remaining close to your left leg whilst you change from normal to fast and back to normal, introduce the change whilst walking in a straight line.

At this point ALWAYS change back to normal pace before executing a turn. If you expect your dog to whip round on a turn before he is confident, you may be disappointed and inadvertently administer rather heavy correction. This will make the dog apprehensive and lay the groundwork for lagging.

Teaching the Turns

The Left Turn is the first one which should be introduced. Give the command 'Close' and help the dog by taking the lead back. If the dog has been taught the Basic Movement correctly the momentum of fast pace usually makes him use his hindquarters correctly.

The Right and Right-about-Turns should be introduced when the Left Turn has been mastered. Again the command is 'Close' and the right hand should come across the body onto the lead and guide the dog round with your left leg.

Praise release and play immediately after each turn whilst the dog is learning.

Slow Heelwork

Slow pace is unnatural and boring for the dog and demands tremendous concentration. Never attempt slow pace until the dog is performing accurately at normal and fast paces.

Once more return to the invaluable figure of eight. Have your dog working happily with his attention on his toy/carpet.

When your dog is on the outside and you are ready, change smoothly into Slow Pace. Only remain at the Slow Pace for a very short while before returning to normal pace and then go into Fast Pace.

This is done to prevent the dog from becoming bored or anxious. Keep plenty of excitement in your voice.

Praise release and play.

Continue as for fast pace introducing the change whilst walking in a straight line.

Introduce Slow Pace into your formal heelwork, always returning to normal before turning. Keep the stretches of Slow Pace very short.

The turns should be introduced as for Fast Pace, giving the command 'Close' and helping the dog by using the lead.

Because of the lack of momentum at Slow Pace the dog probably will not execute the Left Turn correctly. Do not accept a half-hearted turn. Take your dog back with the lead and your left leg and carry out the Basic Movement.

Praise release and play immediately after every turn.

Introducing Change of Pace from the Halt

Have the dog working happily and make one or two changes of pace on the move.

Halt at normal pace. Giving the command 'close' ease into fast pace gradually increasing the speed. As soon as the dog takes a good position Praise release and play. Continue in this manner until the dog moves off confidently at either normal or fast pace. Only then introduce Slow Pace from a halt.

Avoid overturning by keeping your head up as you go into the turns, and look at something straight ahead of you as you come out of the turn. Never turn back towards your dog.

If he does not come with you at Fast Pace bring him up with short firm jerks on the lead. When he is in the correct position execute a Right Turn and Praise release and play.

If the dog surges forward execute a left or left-about turn. Continue for a few paces at *normal* pace. When the dog is in the correct position Praise release and play.

Make allowances at Slow Pace for the dog's lack of understanding. If the dog jumps up it could be because of one of the following causes: (a) Anxiety, (b) Loss of attention, (c) Keenness.

If you have problem (a), slightly quicken your Slow Pace so that it is somewhere between normal and slow. When the dog relaxes at this pace you can gradually slow it down.

If you have problem (b) or (c), give the command 'Close' and using the lead execute a Right Turn, take a few paces at the Slow Pace and Halt. Praise release and play.

The Regulations for heelwork in Class C as laid down by the Kennel Club in January 1985, are as follows:

The dog shall be required to work heel free, and also be tested at fast and slow pace. At some time during this test, at the discretion of the Judge, the dog shall be required, whilst walking to heel at normal pace, to be left at the Stand, Sit and Down in any order (the order to be the same for each dog) as and when directed by the Judge. The handler shall continue forward alone, without hesitation, and continue as directed by the Judge until he reaches his dog when both shall continue forward together until halted. Heelwork may include left about turns and figures of eight at normal and/or slow pace.

By courtesy of the Kennel Club.

13

Positions on the Move

These positions must be taught ONE AT A TIME, on the lead and at a slowish pace. The dog already knows the commands for the positions as he will have learnt them for Distant Control.

Positions on the Move

First Exercise   The Sit Position

1 With your dog on the lead and the lead in your Right Hand, work at a slowish pace.

2 When you have your dog's full attention execute a Left Turn.

3 As you do so give the command 'Sit', pushing him into the Sit position with your left hand on his hindquarters. At the same time tighten the lead with an upward movement of your right hand.

4 Stand by your dog's side and praise him.

5 Release and play.

DO NOT PROGRESS UNTIL YOUR DOG IMMEDIATELY TAKES UP THE SIT POSITION WITHOUT ASSISTANCE.

Second Exercise

Make the same preparation as before. Execute a Left Turn and as you do so give the command 'Sit'. As soon as the dog is sitting, steadily take a step forwards and backwards. If the dog remains steady Praise release and play. If the dog moves release and repeat the first exercise.

Positions on the Move

Third Exercise

1 Make the same preparation as before.

Execute a Left Turn at the same time giving the command 'Sit'. →

and return to the Heel position. →

2 When the dog is sitting

walk round him

3 Praise release and play.

Fourth Exercise

Have the dog walking at normal pace with the lead in your left hand. When you have your dog's full attention execute a Left Turn giving the command 'Sit'. As soon as the dog is sitting drop the lead over the dog's back and leave him making a small left handed circle. Return to the dog's side. Praise release and play.

Fifth Exercise

Proceed as in the fourth exercise until you have dropped the lead then walk off in a forward direction for a few paces, about turn and walk back past your dog for a few paces. About turn and halt at the dog's side.

Praise release and play.

When the dog can execute the fifth exercise into the Sit position reliably and confidently, proceed to teach the Down position.

Positions on the Move

First exercise The Down Position

1 Have the dog on the lead and the lead in the Left hand. Work the dog at a slowish pace.

2 When you have the dog's full attention, execute a Left-about turn.

3 Take the dog back with the basic movement,

at the same time giving the command 'Down'. Continue the movement of the left hand downwards

easing the dog into the Down position. Remain by the dog's side.

4 Praise release and play.

Positions on the Move

Second Exercise

1 Have the dog on the lead and the lead in the left hand. Work the dog at a slowish pace.

2 When you have the dog's full attention, execute a Left-about turn. Take the dog back with the basic movement, at the same time giving the command 'Down'. Continue

→

3 When the dog is in the Down position walk round him and return to the Heel position.

→

the movement of the left hand downwards

easing the dog into the Down position.

4 Praise release and play.

Positions on the Move

First Exercise The Stand Position

With the dog on the lead and the lead in the Right hand, work the dog at a slowish pace until you have his full attention. Execute a Right Turn, at the same time giving the dog's name.

Halt on your right leg and use your left leg under your dog to stop his back legs from moving forwards. Place the open palm of your left hand smartly in front of the dog's muzzle.

Remain stationary by the dog's side for a few seconds. Praise release and play. Do not progress until the dog immediately stops in the stand on being given his name and the signal from the left hand, without any assistance.

When the dog stops and remains steady in the Stand position continue as for the Sit position with exercises 2 through to 5 but always making a Right turn as your give the command.

If the dog breaks position return quickly to his side. Give verbal correction, e.g., 'What are you doing?' Repeat the command for the position and replace him in it. Immediately Praise release and play. Then repeat the exercise.

When the dog can be taken through exercise 5 reliably in all three positions, give one position, collect him and carry on with the heelwork, sometimes giving a second position before releasing.

I very rarely carry out all three positions during a training session as it is not necessary. However I always finish a training session with some heelwork which includes some Left turns without giving a position.

In Conclusion

I set out to attempt to make this book both informative and enjoyable.

I do hope you have found it so because then it will have made the six years it has taken to produce well worth while. The most difficult facet of writing the book has been, I feel, to try to get across to you, the reader, my mannerisms as well as my training methods.

I felt it important for you to appreciate the development needs and capabilities of the young puppy through to adulthood, and indeed your own capabilities.

I felt it equally important to highlight as much detail as possible to show the dangers of cuttings corners which would result in you over-facing your dog, and the need to intersperse the training with lengthy stretches of play so that above all you and your dog would love, work, and grow together.

Kennel Club Regulations for Tests for Obedience Classes S (2)

PART I

PRE-BEGINNERS – Pre-beginners Classes may only be scheduled at Limited and Sanction Obedience Shows. If owner or handler or dog have won a first prize in any Class they may not compete in Pre-Beginners.

Handlers will not be penalised for encouragement or extra commands except in the Sit and Down tests. In these tests, at the discretion of the Judge, handlers may face their dogs. Judges or Stewards must not use the words 'last command' except in the Sit and Down tests.

1 Heel on lead 15 pts
2 Heel free 20 pts
3 Recall from sit or down position at handler's choice. Dog to be recalled by handler when stationary and facing the dog. Dog to return smartly to the handler, sit in front, go to heel – all on command of Judge or Steward to handler. Distance at discretion of Judge. Test commences when handler leaves dog. 10 pts
4 Sit one minute, handler in sight 10 pts
5 Down two minutes, handler in sight 20 pts

TOTAL 75 pts

BEGINNERS – If owner or handler or dog have won a total of two or more first prizes in the Beginners Class, they may not compete in Beginners. Winners of one first prize in any other Obedience Class are ineligible to compete in this Class.

Handlers will not be penalised for encouragement or extra commands except in the Sit and Down tests. In these tests, at the discretion of the Judge, handlers may face their dogs. Judges or Stewards must not use the words 'last command' except in the Sit and Down tests.

1 Heel on lead 15 pts
2 Heel free 20 pts
3 Recall from sit or down position at handler's choice. Dog to be recalled by handler when stationary and facing the dog. Dog to return smartly to handler, sit in front, go to heel – all on command of Judge or Steward to handler. Distance at discretion of Judge. Test commences when handler leaves dog. 10 pts
4 Retrieve any article. Handlers may use their own article. 25 pts
5 Sit one minute, handler in sight 10 pts
6 Down two minutes, handler in sight 20 pts

TOTAL 100 pts

NOVICE – For dogs that have not won two first prizes in Obedience Classes (Beginners Class excepted).

Handlers will not be penalised for encouragement or extra commands except in the Sit and Down tests. In these tests, at the discretion of the Judge, handlers may face their dogs. Judges or Stewards must not use the words 'last command' except in the Sit and Down tests.

1 Temperament Test. To take place immediately before heel on lead. Dog to be on lead in the Stand position, handler to stand by dog. Judge to approach quietly from the front and to run his hand gently down the dog's back. Judge may talk quietly to reassure it. Any undue resentment, cringing, growling or snapping to be penalised. This is not a stand for examination or a stay test. 10 pts
2 Heel on lead 10 pts
3 Heel free 15 pts
4 Recall from sit or down position at handler's choice. Dog to be recalled by handler when stationary and facing the dog. Dog to return smartly to handler, sit in front, go to heel – all on command of Judge or Steward to handler. Distance at discretion of Judge. Test commences when handler leaves dog. 10 pts
5 Retrieve a dumb-bell. Handlers may use their own dumb-bells 15 pts
6 Stand one minute, handler in sight 10 pts
7 Sit one minute, handler in sight 10 pts
8 Down three minutes, handler in sight 20 pts

TOTAL 100 pts

CLASS A – For dogs which have not won three first prizes in Classes A, B and Open ClassC in total.

Simultaneous command and signal will be permitted. Extra commands or signals must be penalised.

1 Heel on lead 15 pts
2 Temperament Test. Will take place before Heel free. Dog to be in the stand position and off lead. Handler to stand beside dog. Conditions as for Novice Temperament Test, except that test will commence with order 'last command' and end with order 'Test finished'. Extra commands will be penalised. This is not a stand for examination or a stay test. 10 pts
3 Heel free 10 pts
4 Recall from Sit or Down position at handler's choice. Dog to be recalled to heel by handler, on command of Judge or Steward, whilst handler is walking away from dog, both to continue forward until ordered to halt. The recall and halt points to be the same for each dog and handler. Test commences following handler's last command to dog. 15 pts
5 Retrieve a dumb-bell. Handlers may use their own dumb-bells. 15 pts
6 Stand two minutes, handler in sight 10 pts
7 Sit two minutes, handler in sight 10 pts
8 Down five minutes, handler out of sight 30 pts
9 Scent Discrimination, handler's scent on Judge's article. The total number of articles shall not exceed ten, all of which shall be clearly visible to the dog. 30 pts

TOTAL 150 pts

PART II

CLASS B – For dogs which have not won three first prizes in Class B and Open Class C in total.

One commanded by word or signal, except in Test 2. Extra commands or signals must be penalised.

1 Heel free. The dog shall be required to walk at heel free and shall also be tested at fast and slow pace. Each change of pace shall commence from the 'halt position'. 30 pts
2 Send Away, Drop and Recall. On command of Judge to handler, dog to be sent away in direction indicated by Judge. After the dog has been dropped, handler will call the dog to heel whilst walking where directed by Judge and both will continue forward until ordered to halt. No obstacle to be placed in path of dog. Simultaneous command and signal is permitted, but as soon as the dog leaves the handler, the arm must be dropped. (N.B. an extra command may be simultaneous command and signal, but must be penalised). 40 pts
3 Retrieve any one article provide by the Judge, but which must not be in any manner injurious to the dog (excluding food or glass). The article to be picked up easily by any breed of dog in that Class

and to be clearly visible to the dog. A separate similar article to be used for each dog. Test commences following Judge or Steward's words 'last command' to handler. 30 pts

4 Stand two minutes, handler out of sight 15 pts
5 Sit two minutes, handler out of sight 15 pts
6 Down ten minutes, handler out of sight 40 pts
7 Scent Discrimination. Handler's scent on article provided by Judge. A separate similar article to be used for each dog and the total number of articles shall not exceed ten, all of which shall be clearly visible to the dog and shall be similar to the article given to the handler. Judges must use a separate similar scent decoy or decoys for each dog. No points will be awarded if the article is given to the dog. 30 pts

TOTAL 200 pts

CLASS C – At Championship Shows: for dogs which have been placed on at least one occasion not lower than third in each Class of Novice Class, Class A, Class B and have won Open Class C with not less than 290 marks on one occasion and have gained at least 290 marks in Open Class C on three further occasions under different Judges. Dogs which qualified for entry in Championship Class C prior to 1st May, 1980 are also eligible.

At Limited and Sanction Shows: Open to all dogs except Obedience Certificate winners and dogs which have obtained any award that counts towards the title of Obedience Champion or the equivalent thereof under the rules of any governing body recognised by the Kennel Club.

One commanded by word or signal, except in Test 2 where an extra command may be simultaneous command and signal. Extra commands or signals must be penalised.

1 Heel work. The dog shall be required to walk at heel free, and also be tested at fast and slow pace. At some time during this test, at the discretion of the Judge, the dog shall be required, whilst walking to heel at normal pace, to be left at the Stand, Sit and Down position in any order (the order to be the same for each dog) as and when directed by the Judge. The handler shall continue forward alone, without hesitation, and continue as directed by the Judge until reaching the dog, when both shall continue forward together until halted. Heel work may include left about turns and figure-of-eight at normal and/or slow pace. 60 pts
2 Send Away, Drop and Recall as in Class B 40 pts
3 Retrieve any one article provided by the Judge but which must not be in any manner injurious to the dog (excluding food or glass). The article to be picked up easily by any breed of dog in that class and to be clearly visible to the dog.

A separate similar article to be used for each dog. Test commances following Judge or Steward's 'last command' to handler. 30 pts

4 Distant Control. Dog to Sit, Stand and Down at a marked place not less than ten paces from handler, in any order on command from Judge to handler. Six instructions to be given in the same order for each dog. Excessive movement, i.e. more than the length of the dog, in any direction by the dog, having regard to its size, will be penalised. The dog shall start the exercise with its front feet behind a designated point. No penalty for excessive movement in a forward direction shall be imposed until the back feet of the dog pass the designated point. 50 pts
5 Sit two minutes, handler out of sight 20 pts
6 Down ten minutes, handler out of sight 50 pts
7 Scent Discrimination. Judge's scent on a piece of marked cloth. Neutral and decoy cloths to be provided by the Show Executive. The Judge shall not place his cloth in the ring himself, but it shall be placed by a Steward. A separate similar piece to be used for each dog and the total number of separate similar pieces of cloth from which the dog shall discriminate shall not exceed ten. If a dog fetches or fouls a wrong article this must be replaced by a fresh-article. At open-air shows all scent cloths must be adequately weighted to prevent them being blown about. The method of taking scent shall be at the handler's discretion, but shall not require the Judge to place his hand on or lean towards the dog. A separate similar piece of cloth approximately 6 inches by 6 inches but not more than 10 inches shall be available to be used for giving each dog the scent. Judges should use a scent decoy or decoys. 50 pts

TOTAL 300 pts

Potters Bar

1st. & c.c. Mrs S Bishop and Ob. Ch. Enchanted Blue Star (W/S).

This was the first time I have had the pleasure of giving this pair the Ticket (The third this year already I believe). The combination of this great little bitch and her really excellent handler make them a team really hard to beat.

Ruislip/Northwood CTS

1st. Mrs S Bishop – 'Misty Magic' (NAF) (W/S).

The last dog in the class to work and without any question of doubt in my mind this young bitch has more potential than any Novice dog or bitch that I have judged for several years.

Coventry DTC

1st. & OCC. Mrs S Bishop's Ob. Ch. Enchanted Blue Star (W/S).

Finishing two clear points ahead of the field speaks for itself. I gave them absolutely nothing and one spectator had the decency to applaud the round. My congratulations on your fifth ticket this year and on producing, technically, one of the finest rounds of precision obedience I have yet seen.

Normanton DFC – Pontefract Racecourse

1st. Mrs S Bishop and Magic Sunday (W/S).

I can only re-iterate Bill Pykett's recent remarks when awarding this team their first ticket at Leicester GSD Club. A super partnership who many try to emulate and end up envying. An exceptional round to watch and judge.

Guide Dog Show

1st. Mrs S Bishop's Misty Magic WSD.

A clear round and undoubtedly the best round of the day. It was quite a remarkable performance for an 18 month old bitch. What a pleasure it was to see the joy and excitement of the handler at this win in spite of the fact that she must have won so many first prizes before.

Epsom

3rd. Mrs S Bishop's Magic Sunday W/S.

Much is said about this handler and her dogs. This latest whizz-kid is poetry in motion, achieved by an understanding of dogs that is most enviable.